MORE WORDS

More Words

Dannie Abse
Eleanor Bron
R. W. Burchfield
Robert Conquest
Margaret Drabble
Christopher Driver
D. J. Enright
John Fletcher
Stephen Hearst
David Martin
Chaim Raphael
Frederic Raphael
Cardew Robinson
Ian Robinson
Vernon Scannell
Kenneth Tynan
Mary Warnock
John Weightman
John Ziman

British Broadcasting Corporation

Published by the
British Broadcasting Corporation
35 Marylebone High Street
London W 1 M 4 A A

I S B N 0 563 17298 3

First published 1977

Printed in England by
Tonbridge Printers Ltd
Peach Hall Works, Shipbourne Road
Tonbridge, Kent

Contents

Foreword

Language, as an instrument of precise expression and clear thought, has had a bad time in the last ten or twenty years. Romanticism holds sway over classicism, feeling over thinking. In the ideological battles of our time, language itself has come under attack as a subtle tool of the dominant classes. Opposed ideological camps have found it greatly to their advantage to wrest the sole use of words endowed with particular political or cultural magic from each other. Observe, for example, the patient repetition of 'democratic' as in 'German Democratic Republic' by Eastern European countries, thus making its confident use by the West much more difficult. Or note how in internal British struggles the word 'élite', used not so long ago with pride by those who thought they belonged to it and enviously by others who felt they did not, has lately become a tool of aggressive linguistic contempt. Theft of linguistic meaning is practised on a large scale and there is no law to prevent it.

Those of us who care about language as perhaps the finest tool of civilisation are further handicapped by the prodigious spread of a visual electronic culture, television. When the average family viewing time in the United States amounts, as it does, to six hours per day and in Britain to nearly three hours, it becomes permissible, even for a television producer by profession like myself, to point to the emergence, possibly the dominance, of a visual culture. Language necessarily plays second fiddle to images in television and the prolonged daily exposure to the flow of television images may have cultural effects which we have not as yet gauged. At the very least, we ought to work consciously for the continuing health and vitality of our language. Sound radio, with language one of its principal props, has good reason to regard the improvement of linguistic expression as a legitimate objective of public service broadcasting. Thus in a BBC sense may the old world, radio, come to redress the balance of the new.

Not that Radio 3's modest weekly series *Words* would or could lay claim to defend some linguistic inner sanctum. Our language is not to be guarded, as in France, by an academy. New words are born in unexpected places. Yet *Words* does constitute a forum: for love of language, for the expression of linguistic heresy or orthodoxy, for nostalgia, for prejudice; above all, perhaps, for clarity of meaning.

The appearance of *More Words* is partly proof of the success of the previous volume *Words*, partly evidence of the continuing public interest in matters of language. Our contributors include poets, novelists, teachers, journalists, playwrights, actors, editors or rather unclassifiable tasters, consumers, practitioners and defenders of words. They have all helped to prove that it is possible to expound worth-while ideas in under five minutes flat and Radio 3 owes them a debt of gratitude. Not to them alone; two colleagues need to be protected from the short memory of broadcasting and remembered in print: Daniel Snowman, who produced most of these short talks, and George Fischer, whose idea the series *Words* was in the first place.

Stephen Hearst
Controller, Radio 3

Mary Warnock

Writing the spoken word

It is an extraordinarily disconcerting experience to be shown an exact transcript of a conversation you had taken part in. The incoherence, the gaps, the repetitions are all of them most shocking to the eye. But quite apart from actual syntactical chaos, there are some important differences of vocabulary which distinguish spoken language from written language. There are some things you can quite happily say but you would never write; and then there are some things that you can read and write, but never utter. It's funny really how little reflexion you give to this difference; on the whole you just more or less accept it and adapt accordingly. But standards differ, and degrees of formality in written prose and in speech differ too.

˙ I personally hate it when, in rather stiff academic prose, the balance tips too far towards the spoken word. Take the word 'though'. It's becoming common to use this word in written English as one might use it in speech and I find this disagreeable. Now this bit of dialogue, spoken, would be quite acceptable. 'I might ring him up.' 'Yes, you could. It wouldn't be very wise, though, because he hates the telephone.' The 'though' here introduces an objection meant to outweigh the agreement contained in the 'yes'. But objections and counter-arguments are not well introduced by 'though' in written prose. Take this, for instance, 'Some people think that girls should prepare themselves for life by learning cooking at school. There is another argument, though, that cookery classes are an expensive waste of time.' Now I would much prefer 'however' here. Another example, rather a gruesome one, but I've actually seen this written: 'seat-belts usually make driving safer. This driver, though, was killed by his seat-belt.' Now surely we would want 'however' here. 'However' like 'moreover' and 'nevertheless' essentially belongs to written English. Ought we to try to expel such words from written language because they've got no place in speech? I don't think we should. I think there is a lot to be said for keeping a distinction, and keeping the kind of tension it involves. After all a writer can in fact vary his style by bringing it nearer to spoken language or further from it. Obviously if you're writing a novel the ability to do this may be crucially important. But even if he doesn't want to reproduce spoken language, a writer may want to button-hole his reader, to talk to him suddenly more directly than through the medium of formal prose. And he can do this by using his 'thoughs' his 'can'ts' and 'won'ts' and 'isn'ts'. Mind you I hate too much of these too. Nothing is more incongruous than when, after a long philosophical argument, a writer says 'And that isn't all . . . ' and then goes on to another equally complicated argument. It is as if he is trying to ingratiate himself, to make his book seem more readable.

Taste and style, both in writing and in talking, display themselves in the management of this tension, in the search after the mean between the pompous and the slangy, and that's whether we give thought to the search or pursue it instinctively.

Of course, the over-colloquial prose writer may irritate us or displease us. But, in fact, his power over us is not as great as the power of the pompous or 'prosey' speaker. Think of the man who does actually say 'however' or use the word 'moreover' or 'nevertheless'. We know when he does that we're really at his mercy. He is going to make his point, his argument, his counter-argument and qualification though the heavens fall. After all you can shut a book if you don't like it. But with the real 'prosey' speaker you just have to wait until he has had his say and finished it.

A timid vice

Philosophers and theorists of child-development sometimes tell us that we learn the use of abstract words like 'whiteness', 'similarity' or 'antiquity' by seeing and learning to describe a lot of different white objects, or pairs of things which are alike or antiques. More eccentric philosophers like Plato thought that we somehow had to know in advance what whiteness was or we would never have been able to tell that a particular object was white. But even Plato held that there was some connexion between the abstract word and the concrete things which manifest the quality named by the word. But how is it that we can learn to understand abstract words for moral qualities, like 'duty', 'sin', 'evil', 'goodness', 'virtue', 'vice'? Nowadays, although these words are understood and even form the main subject matter that some philosophers and educationalists are concerned with, concrete examples of human character and behaviour are seldom, if ever, described in terms of them. The corresponding descriptive adjectives are hardly used at all. Whoever seriously describes a course of conduct, a thought or a desire as sinful? Whoever thinks of someone's character as virtuous, or his choice as courageous, or his actions as dutiful? There is a mystery here. The concepts picked on by the theorists as essential to morality seem to have no use whatever in ordinary speech. If anyone so much as uses the expression 'morally wrong' you can be almost sure that he's a philosopher with a special technical acquaintance with the term.

Of course it wasn't always like this. At the end of a day of overeating, chasing a pig round the garden and playing on a forbidden swing, the Fairchild family, conceived by Mrs Sherwood in 1818, confess to their father and mother. 'I'm glad that you have told the truth my children,' said Mr Fairchild. 'But the sins that you have committed are very dreadful ones.' And nearly a hundred years later when a schoolgirl was suspected of stealing money, her headmistress visits her, according to Angela Brazil, locked as she is in the music room in her disgrace, and says: 'Don't give way, Raymonde. I for one trust you. Keep your self-control. Remember there is nothing like courage and speaking the truth.' There is no doubt that then people had particular cases of virtue and vice, so described, to help them to acquire the general concepts.

But now we don't hear as much, either in life or in literature, about these moral concepts or their particular exemplifications. Is it that we have no morality left? I doubt that very much. But if we look at the kinds of words we actually use now to praise people or blame them morally, we can see the way things are going. Imagine yourself in a state of moral indignation. You've been cheated, you've seen a child made a fool of, you've discovered some gross exploitation. Or on the other hand you have discovered that someone has made a great sacrifice for you. What do you actually say? For one thing I think we tend to blame people or praise them in terms which are not specifically moral. We use quite general terms like 'marvellous', 'awful', 'ghastly', 'wonderful', that kind of thing. This is a kind of careless talk which is less embarrassing because less committing than specific words like 'courageous' or 'cowardly'. And then again I think we're terrified of anything other than the subjective. We tend to protect ourselves by using a vocabulary which makes everything a matter of taste. If we give advice we tend to say: 'If I were you I'd...', rather than 'you ought to'. We say 'I'm against it' rather than 'It's wrong', or 'It makes me sick' but not 'It's wicked'. Our moral language has become terribly timorous. If we do believe in objective standards, we conceal it. Perhaps for a change we should practise again describing things as right or wrong so that we can revive our sense of general words by reference to these particulars. We don't after all want to lose all notion of the difference between right and wrong, or forget that niceness is actually nicer than nastiness.

Women's words

Words are a bit like clothes. For one thing they're subject to fashion. Last year's word which seemed apt or witty at the time may now seem jejune or vulgar, dated. Words, like clothes, are partly a matter of basic need, but are partly used for decorative or aesthetic purposes. They express the personality or conceal it. I wonder too whether there aren't just possibly sex differences in words, as in clothes. Obviously by far the greatest number of words will fall into the unisex class. But each side of this perhaps there are men's words and women's words. There are, I'm sure, lots of different kinds just as there are lots of kinds of women's clothes. But there's one particular class of words which comes to my mind as women's; words which I used to find irritating, indeed enraging, but which I now find sadly endearing as the mark of a bygone age. I mean the words specially associated with dedicated academic women, either dons or school mistresses, mostly unmarried, devoted to their pupils or to research; career women, but without interest in career-structure, or indeed in financial reward.

Many of the best of these words are to be found still in girls' school reports or headmistresses' letters in the school magazine. Take for instance the word 'multifarious'. How often have we heard about the multifarious activities which have gone on at a school in the past academic year. And then follows a list of the sketching club, the dramatic society, the fencing, the judo, the orchestras, the Guild of Service. The exact force of the word, I suppose, is that it combines 'many' with 'various'. But it's not a word, useful though this combination might be, that one's at all likely to find in a chairman's report to the shareholders, or a civil servant's draft of a committee's recommendations. Another specimen is 'goodly', 'A goodly array' might be the phrase used to describe the fork-supper provided for the old girls' reunion, or for the piles of jumble ready for the charity sale. As so often, the adjective tends to come on dragging a particular noun with it.

'Multifarious activities', 'a goodly array', or of course, 'a goodly heritage'. Note that women's words are often either quotations or somehow echoes of quotations, usually from Shakespeare, the Bible, or the *Book of Common Prayer*. Groups of girls are often characterised as 'the wise or foolish virgins'. 'Right' and 'proper' are nearly always joined together. Jokingly people may be reproved for their 'manifold sins and wickedness'. Between the first and the second division French there is 'a great gulf fixed'.

If we turn to the school report, we find another word, 'pleasing'. 'A pleasing term's work' we read. 'Margaret's biological drawings have been very pleasing'. I can think of no other context in which I could be so sure of finding this particular word. Though it has got no quotation marks round it, it seems to come out of the same somewhat archaic quotation basket as the rest.

The quotation marks used to be audible too, round the words used by women dons in their common rooms if they ever felt obliged to ask their married colleagues about their families. How, they would say, are your 'offspring'? Never children or babies. How I used to fume and rage at 'offspring'. But now it fills me with gentle melancholy. The irony, the quotations, the facetiousness and audible inverted commas – these were all protective clothing ('garments' they would have said, or 'raiment') covering, but not obscuring or confusing, what the users were really, non-ironically, devoted to, which was their pupils and their work. Their clichés never constituted a jargon. They never tried, by words alone, to prove that education was a science. They didn't chatter about 'input', 'integration' or 'interface'. Even 'interdisciplinary' was unheard. It's understandable that one should feel affection for these women's words. It is the new nostalgia.

Chaim Raphael

The Best Kind of Argument

I love an argument, but not the kind that most people think of when they use the word. If you ask somebody: 'What's the best kind of argument – between people who agree or who disagree with each other?' most people instantly plump for the second. The reason seems obvious to them. If one agrees about everything, the talk is bound to be dull. One gets no further than when one began. By contrast, to encounter an opposing view broaden's one's horizons. The 'rapier-thrust of challenge is stimulating' – and so on.

Maybe: but I find it infinitely more rewarding to be talking to someone who agrees with me: or to be more precise, someone who shares some common interests and assumptions. Agreement stimulates one to be flighty, provocative in the *good* sense, imaginative in a way you can't achieve on your own. Talking to someone this way, you may find that you both loved a particular movie and plunge into exchanging the great moments, reliving each one and finding it deeper as you talk. Or you may both have seen through the pretensions of a certain professor and outdo each other in satire or parody, rising to heights that you never dreamed you had in you. Agreement enriches experience.

At the opposite extreme one thinks of those discussions on television – especially on politics – where the exercise is designed to confront two speakers who by definition are going to see nothing whatever in the opposing view. Far from stimulating each other, the talk builds an artificial wall round each person's mind. People often call at election time for a straight debate on television between the two top leaders: but given this built-in sterility, it would surely stand no chance of being rewarding intellectually. How different it would be – can we at least dream about it? – if Mr Wilson and Mr Heath sat down before the cameras assuming that they do, in fact, share a wide common experience and were going to take off from there. 'I liked what you were doing on X,' Mr Wilson might say. 'Why didn't you keep it up?' 'We wanted to,' Mr Heath would reply, 'but the Treasury were against it'. The Treasury! The common enemy! Now they could really take off.

Dreaming of this brings to mind the most distinctive kind of talk ever recorded – Plato's *Dialogues*, especially, perhaps, the *Protagoras*, since this is the one discussion in which Socrates, meeting his doughty Sophist opponent, not only fails for once to get the better of the argument, but never really expects to. What emerges is not a determination of right or wrong, but rather a presentation of two ways of approaching a common issue, both of which embody a certain truth. As Plato describes it, the two men really listen to each other, very ready to see the other's views: indeed they almost switch positions, so free is the talk.

It's not easy to realise this kind of give-and-take in art form, but I can think of two examples that to my mind are perfect.

The first is the character of discussion in the *Talmud*. The rabbis, utterly in agreement on basic issues, are free to argue in the most uninhibited way, quoting this or that authority to enlarge the discussion, agreeing, disagreeing, and sometimes ending up deciding that it's impossible to say who is really right or wrong, and that they will have to leave the final answer to the prophet Elijah when he reappears.

The other example is in music, which is almost always a conversation, especially, somehow, with wind instruments. A favourite example for me is the last movement of Mozart's *Sinfonia Concertante* for oboe, clarinet, horn and bassoon. The theme is stated and then off they go. The oboe speaks, the clarinet says something similar but in his way, the horn joins in rather breathlessly, the bassoon is so ponderous about it that they all have to laugh. They listen to each other, they echo, they wander off, and they come back happily every few minutes to a joint celebration of the common theme. None of them will ever forget what a wonderful argument they have had.

Don't throw your pearls to the pigs

Do you ever use a familiar phrase without thinking and then suddenly ask yourself where it comes from, or what it means – or both? Sometimes you decide that its origin is basically physical, as, for example, 'my heart was in my mouth', or 'my hair stood on end', or 'I screwed up my courage'. But why do we say: 'Stop beating about the bush', or 'I was green with jealousy', or 'I escaped by the skin of my teeth'.

If you try to track down the origins in a reference book, you find that many of these catch-phrases come from the Bible or Shakespeare. With phrases traced to Shakespeare this more or less solves the problem, because the meaning comes out in the context. But what about the phrases we track down to the Bible? The joker here is that they're often not in the Bible at all.

The source for us is, of course, the Authorised Version. When we meet a striking phrase there – so striking that it has forced itself into our daily use – we assume that this reflects the genius of the original. In fact, however, it's often an invention – but a marvellous one – of the translators, usually because they had no idea what the text in front of them really meant.

A typical example of this is the original, in Job, of 'the skin of my teeth'. For us, this means a narrow shave. But Job isn't saying this. He's describing the effect on him of his desertion by everybody. It's made him feel physically ill. The full verse runs, in the Authorised Version: 'My bone cleaveth to my skin and to my flesh, and I am escaped with the skin of my teeth'. It doesn't really make any sense in English, because it's a word-by-word translation of a Hebrew text which has obviously got corrupted. Modern scholars, who accept that the Bible text isn't perfect as it stands, have tried modifying the words and moving them round to yield something that fits the context. It's amazing how many variants they've suggested, getting funnier and funnier to our ears, such as 'In my skin, my flesh has rotted away and I have gnawed my bone to the teeth'. Another one is: 'My flesh rots on my bones: my teeth drop from my gums'. But it's no good. 'Skin of my teeth' has forced itself into our language over the centuries, and we 'escape' by it.

Job is full of this. There's the famous verse: 'Man is born to trouble as the sparks fly upward'. The original Hebrew is extremely mysterious mainly because the word they translated as 'sparks' is *reshef*, which is in fact the name of a Pheonician God that the translators had never heard of. But we still prefer to be stuck with those sparks.

The reason is that once a writer with a gift for poetry has created a living phrase, it's this that matters, and not some original text. The most famous example of this is: 'Yea though I walk through the valley of the shadow of death I fear no evil'. We now know that 'shadow of death' is a totally wrong translation. This three-word phrase is, in the Hebrew text, only one word which has been split up incorrectly and really means 'deep darkness'. Even the word 'valley' is questioned by the scholars, and the sentence probably means literally: 'Even if I go through the deepest darkness . . .', which, in fact, is how the *Good News Bible* translates it.

The *New English Bible* tries to compromise by saying 'Through a valley dark as death' – a really silly change which tries to be traditional but gives up the traditional poetry.

It's as if the N.E.B. translators have no ear. In their version, 'casting pearls before swine' becomes: 'Do not throw your pearls to the pigs'. I turned the page to see what they'd done with 'a camel going through the eye of a needle,' a delightful phrase that we'd surely hate to lose. It really means: 'It is easier for a camel to get through a narrow "eye of a needle" gate than for a rich man to enter heaven'. The new translators might have tried some awful paraphrase, but thank goodness: they've left the old words unimproved.

Vernon Scannell

Mizzled magic

I was born in 1922 so my childhood was spent during the depression years of the twenties and thirties. My parents were hard up and I wasn't bright enough – or bright enough in the right way – to be given a place at the grammar school so I had to put up with an ordinary elementary education which ended when I was fourteen. Now from my earliest years I was passionately fond of reading and from the time I was about twelve I was determined to be a writer. Words fascinated me. There was a snag though: I wasn't always sure how the words should really sound because my acquaintance with them had been made nearly always on the page and many of them I'd never actually heard spoken at all. We didn't possess what was then called a wireless until I was in my early teens and even when we did acquire one the only programmes I heard were news broadcasts, sports commentaries, or music hall comedians and singers. There was no Third Programme then and, even if there had been, I doubt if I'd have heard it at home. In fact I was not only given no guide to pronunciation of my beloved words, I was positively misguided. My father, for instance, often used a word 'mizzled' by which he meant deceived or led astray and when I came across the word 'misled' on the printed page I instantly recognised it as 'mizzled' and I pronounced it like that for some years before somebody put me right.

There is, by the way, such a word as 'mizzled' and a very pleasing word it is too. It's the past tense of 'to mizzle', a dialect word of the fifteenth century which means to drizzle rain. And there is also, according to the *Shorter Oxford English Dictionary*, an eighteenth-century slang word 'mizzle' and this means to disappear suddenly. You can see easily enough how the first mizzle came into existence – it adds the visuality of mistiness to the onomatopoeia of drizzle. 'Mizzle' – to disappear suddenly – might belong to the same family as 'whizz' and 'fizzle' and it's just possible that it could be related to 'mizzy'; that's a word deriving from Old English meaning a bog or quagmire into which things might disappear fairly rapidly.

But to get back to what I was saying about acquiring a vocabulary simply through private reading: I was often mizzled – I mean misled – by the appearance of a word, and its relation to other words in a phrase or sentence. I remember at school proudly using the word salubrious in a composition to describe a row of cramped and squinting little houses in a midland slum. I wasn't merely surprised but almost disbelieving when my teacher told me I must have mistaken the meaning of the word. To me it sounded so grim, so unhealthy, with its strong echo of lugubrious and the sallowness of its first syllable.

Still, I don't feel too severely deprived by my lack of formal education though I do regret my almost total ignorance of Latin and Greek. I think I get at least as much excitement and pleasure from my explorations into the English language as many more efficiently equipped travellers if only because I'm constantly being thrilled and surprised by suddenly seeing relations between words which I'd never before suspected. Language still holds for me a good deal of the magic that I felt so powerfully as a child and it's possible that some of this might be dispersed if my knowledge were more thorough and scientific. While words remain for me strange, mysterious, vital things, infinitely surprising, infinitely exciting, the possibility is always there – or so it seems to me – that I might one day write a poem that will be informed itself by the spirit of language, a poem that will be strange, mysterious, vital and packed with meaning.

The vigour of abuse

About twenty years ago I wrote a first novel about the fight
game – or, as we in England would say, professional boxing
– and I found that the sedateness and urbanity of English
just couldn't handle the toughness, and grittiness, the sweat
and action of my subject. When a language is in a state of
robust health, exuberantly aware of itself and growing
almost daily richer and stronger, as English was in the
sixteenth and seventeenth centuries, the vigour of ordinary
speech is bound to be found also in the literature of the time.
The American language of the present century, both literary
and colloquial, is enjoying something like the vigorous
health of Elizabethan and Jacobean English, and our language, well it's rather lacking in that earlier flexibility and
energy. In England politicians 'stand' for office. In America
they 'run'.

One of the sure proofs of the vitality of a language can be
found in the energy of its vernacular invective. Here, modern
English – and not only the speech of the middle and upper
classes – is conspicuously feeble compared with American. If
you look at the plays of Shakespeare, Webster, Ben Jonson
and the lesser Elizabethan dramatists or the prose say of
Thomas Nashe or Robert Burton, the contemporary invective
was not only vivid, aggressive and tremendously hard-
hitting, it was strikingly like the American spoken language
of abuse – brawny, brutal, merciless. The Americans often
make use of compound words that seem directly descended
from the Elizabethans. 'Sonofabitch' – and this is a relatively
mild one – is obviously very close in shape and tone to the
Elizabethan 'whoresondog' but it would be impossible for a
twentieth-century Englishman to echo language like this
without sounding absurd. Apart from the mechanical and
monotonous obscenities of barrack-room, gaol and criminal
underworld, the British arsenal of verbal abuse is ill-
furnished.

The vigour, the physical strength and economy of the

American language has been of immense help to those writers who take for their subject physical action and sensation of a violent kind. I can think of no modern British writer who can equal Hemingway at the business of communicating the immediate sense of what it feels like to be involved in strenuous and dangerous physical activity or, for that matter, one who can convey the taste, the touch, and the smell and feel of things nearly so well as he. And all those American popular crime writers of the tough school who learnt directly or indirectly from Hemingway, they are incomparably better at their job than our thriller writers. Compared with, say, Chandler, Hammett, John D. MacDonald, Patricia Highsmith, writers like Leslie Charteris, Dick Francis and Agatha Christie seem woefully limp and genteel. And this isn't only because they have no Hemingway to serve as exemplar; it's because they haven't the same language of violence to call on.

Still, all is not lost for the British writer. The muscularity, the natural forcefulness of American speech rhythms and idioms are ill-suited when it comes to dealing with more tender and subjective matters, while the cadence and diction of English speech lend themselves to the reflective and the lyrical, also to a special kind of wit that is inimitably of this island. The British writer must capitalise on his limitations, box clever, and leave the brawling to the Americans. We can do with both. It would be as hard to imagine an American Evelyn Waugh as it would an English Norman Mailer and I know which one I would choose to preserve if one of them had to go.

Romantic lawn mowers

The old controversies which commanded a lot of attention during the time of Wordsworth and Coleridge about the nature of poetic diction don't seem to be of much interest to modern literary critics and I would guess that most people who're at all concerned with poetry would agree that the poet is free to use any word at all as long as it works in its context. The idea that certain words out of context are in themselves beautiful or 'poetic', and others not, would be rejected by most poets and critics alive now. Certainly I would disagree vehemently with the idea expressed quite often – though rarely by poets themselves – that there is such a thing as pure verbal music, that one can enjoy a poem without understanding the words, just for the lovely noise it makes when read aloud. I don't believe – taken as pure sound – any word can be called more beautiful than another. Perhaps certain onomatopoeic words, such as 'squelch' or 'murmur', whose meaning is their sound, could be called ugly or beautiful, but I'm not entirely sure about this. What I am sure of is that, to anyone totally unaware of the meanings of, say, 'syphilis' and 'syllables', neither word would be more or less attractive than the other. However, once the meanings and associations of a given word are part of one's experience, it's then impossible to divorce sound from significance, so words can, even out of context, arouse responses of delight, revulsion, sadness and gaiety.

Take the word 'melancholy'. I imagine that to all of us it conjures up feelings – perhaps in some of us definite visual images – of gloom, sadness, depression, and the sense of darkness will almost certainly be present even for those who don't know that 'melancholy' derives from the Greek meaning 'black bile'. Yet I'd guess that many people, perhaps most, would say that it is an agreeable, perhaps a beautiful word. Its unlovely origins don't alter the fact that 'melancholy' has acquired strong romantic associations and I suspect that few people today would react with revulsion to the word, though many might have done before the time of the Romantics. Milton, you will remember, begins *L'Allegro* with:

'Hence loathed melancholy,
Of Cerberus and blackest midnight born,
In Stygian cave forlorn,
'Mongst horrid shapes, and shrieks, and sights unholy.'

Melancholy was loathsome and it wasn't until nearly 200 years later that Keats enthroned romantic 'melancholy' in his ode. Keats makes direct comment on the beauty of the isolated word when, in *Ode to a Nightingale*, he says:

'Forlorn! the very word is like a bell
To toll me back from thee to my sole self . . . '

But obviously 'forlorn' was not like a bell to Milton when he wrote of:

' . . . Stygian cave forlorn,
'Mongst horrid shapes and shrieks and sights unholy.'

He was using the word in its sense of desolate, hopeless and wretched – incidentally, 'forlorn' derives from an Old English word meaning 'to lose, destroy or cause to perish'. 'Forlorn, the very word is like a bell . . . ' yes, perhaps it is, in the context of the ode, but it's a funeral bell, a melancholy sound as the pattern of rhythms, images and associations, insists.

The pure word-music boys might claim that Keats' lines support their belief that the sounds of certain words are aesthetically delightful, that 'forlorn', irrespective of its sense, is a beautiful sound. I think not. I believe that, when they hear the word, they unconsciously supply a context derived from their previous experience of the word and for a literate person in the twentieth century it will be a romantic context. Place the sound – not necessarily the word, but an almost identical sound – in a different and unromantic context, in an advertisement for lawn-mowers for example, and the sound would no longer be beautiful and haunting. It wasn't then, was it, when I said '*for lawn* mowers'?

Robert Conquest

Languishing monosyllables

It is difficult to exhaust the versatility of words. Our language is cunning past belief. Consider, for example, those words which indicate as yet non-existent objects, or gain their force only when they are omitted, or (a broader category) are in most people's vocabulary but are only regarded as usable in special social circumstances.

First, then, that curious category of words which are by quite widespread convention used about objects which have not yet come into being. The side-arm of the future is (not invariably, but over a very wide range of science fiction) continually called the 'blaster'. The currency of the future, again, is that not yet existent coin the 'credit'.

Then, what about the verbal effect of words which are not there at all. Quantum theory developed forty-odd years ago the concept of 'holes' – localised absences of matter, which had what amounted to physical properties. Similarly, on occasion, with language. I cannot remember who it was that pointed out to me a very curious army usage, the omissive emphatic. It is a matter of the present participle of the most widely used word in the forces, which the BBC would prefer not to inflict on you. A case in point would be the fairly slow and easy movement of men when the sergeant shouts 'Get your *blanking* rifles!', compared with the desperate urgency produced by the omission of this normal automatic qualifier, when he says just, 'Get your rifles!'

Which leads us to that very significant group of words, the obscene ones commonly called Anglo-Saxon. There have always been periods which have used words previously regarded as obscene with greater freedom than the generation before – though they have equally often been succeeded by generations which have reversed the process. All the same, until now at any rate, obscene words had a particular quality: there was, as it were, a pool of them, sometimes large, sometimes small, which had one definite characteristic. The words concerned were not used in every sort of company. There are nowadays (and have been for a decade or two) mirror image puritans who want – as they suppose – to liberate these languishing monosyllables from the constraints put upon them by wordist pigs. But of course, in fact, this sort of verbal egalitarianism impoverishes rather than enriches a language. A group of words with special characteristics is simply merged into the rest of our speech, a whole special mode ceases to exist. Or such would appear to be the intention of the liberators.

It has not, in fact, worked out that way. There are certain types of company – gatherings of great aunts, say, or nuns – in which only two sorts of person would employ the four-letter vocabulary: the fanatic who has made it a principle to do so on all occasions, and the fool (usually young) who has been confused by the fanatic's propaganda, or for other reasons has failed to grasp the nuances of language as a social vehicle.

Incidentally there are plenty of progressives who are, if anything, more opposed to this sort of thing than most right-wingers – as with both the methodist and the maoist traditions in the English left. A curious example of this came my way quite recently. In a letter to the *New Statesman* I quoted (with his permission) a characterisation Philip Larkin once wrote me, in a private letter, of the Eastern European Communist leaders: 'dreary, no-good, *blanks*'. The actual word (which on this occasion has been omitted at my own insistence, not that of the BBC) implies that its objects are contemptible as well as unpleasant. Those who know this poet's subtle ear should be able to restore the original. I was rung up to say that they could not print 'that word'. I said that in that case I would be happy if they put XXX in instead, but they said they couldn't do that either. My interpretation – it is hard to think of any other – is that to have printed the word would have offended their puritanical idealists, to have openly failed to print it would have offended their anti-censorship idealists.

Either way, a healthy respect for the power of words was evident, and I hope, whatever your views, that you can scarce forbear to cheer.

A living index of history

Velunia, Volitanio, Pexa, Begesse, Colanica, Medionemeton, Subdobiadon, Litana, Cibra, Credigone . . .

These words are the names of the forts of the Antonine Wall built by the Romans from Forth to Clyde; or rather, of some of the forts. With a single exception, we don't quite know which. They constitute the sort of problem I personally find extraordinarily interesting and tantalising. In my view, Colanica must be Camelon, but I won't burden you with my theories; and speak instead of the layer upon layer of places and place-names where 'seven sunken Englands lie buried one by one'.

The place-names I mentioned are, in fact, dead ones, which may however yet be identified with particular ruins. In the place-names we actually use today, we are equally taken back to different levels of our island's history and culture, to words, or variants on words, which were used by our remotest ancestors for their homes and landscapes. They form a living index of the nation's history. Epoch upon epoch, people upon people, are represented. There are even a few still existing names which are evidently pre-Celtic – the River Stour, for example.

Place names, it is true, have accumulated a good deal of

erroneous folk etymology and various other mistakes – most of them due to enthusiastic amateur antiquarians around the eighteenth century. Our word Mancunian, which it's far too late to get rid of, is based on a misunderstanding of the Roman name of Manchester, which was really Mamucium. It is even difficult to get rid of alleged ancient place names simply invented by the famous forger Bertram.

On the other hand, it isn't always certain what the name's origin is, which gives fantasy many an opening. This applies even in America. When I lived in Buffalo I was often told that the word had nothing to do with the animal, but was derived from Beau fleuve: that is the Niagara River. There are people here who will tell you that Shotover is derived from Château Vert.

Actually, I find genuine books on place names rather tiring after a bit, even though it is always pleasant to come across things like the fact that Beaumont in Essex was a Norman-French cleaning-up of an original Saxon name meaning 'foul pit'.

I prefer, though, to think about the genuine, yet more romantic perspective. It is both a pleasure and an exercising of the muscles of the imagination to consider the ancientness of names like Thames and Avon, Dover and Carlisle, Kent and Devon, going back to pre-Roman times. You might try the time-wasting parlour game of finding which counties of England have pre-English names, and which English. Not as easy as it sounds. The same can be done for the States of America – which are Indian, which European. And, speaking of America, another set of names which fills me with overpowering curiosity, are the place names given by the Norsemen to various points on the North American continent: Markland, Keelness, Wonderstrands, and so on. These are clearly described, and there is no doubt at all that they represent genuine locations. But which? The weight of opinion is that Keelness is Cape Cod: but this is disputed and there are several other candidates.

These, like those of the Antonine Wall with which I started, are names no longer in use. We find them fossilised in the sources – themselves splendidly evocative words: *The Tale of the Greenlanders, The Saga of Eric the Red.* Come to that, consider the sources for the Roman names in the area of the two walls: the *Ravenna Cosmography*, the *Antonine Itinerary*, the *Notitia Dignitatum*, the Amiens Skillet, the Rudge Cup. And of course, inscriptions on stone of the exotic regiments garrisoning them and of the famous Legions of the Army of Britain who actually built them – the Second Augusta, the Sixth Victrix and the Twentieth Valeria Victrix. Place-names, book-names, regimental-names – extinct or still in use – these proper nouns sound good and are splendid to say. But they may also seduce us into serious thinking about our world and its past.

Ruined by revolution

I think it would be fair to call ours the age of word-fetishism.

In her memoirs, Nadezhda Mandelstam, widow of the great Russian poet who perished in the Stalin purges, remarked that a whole generation of Russian intellectuals were ruined by the word 'revolution'.

For more than fifty years before 1917, 'revolution' had meant more than the mere concept of abrupt political or social change. In a society with no civic tradition, no practice of political reality, the future presented itself – as it did in the old slave empires – as leading to a transcendental event in which the old tyranny would be destroyed and a new heaven would triumphantly emerge. What actually happened, when the time came, clearly had every right to call itself revolution. It was carried out by revolutionaries. It produced total change. So, even if everything in practice seemed worse than before rather than better, the idea made manifest, the word, could not be gainsaid.

In Britain, except in very limited circles indeed, the word 'revolution' in itself has never had quite that status. It has been for us rather the sort of thing the French do without gaining any apparent advantage over ourselves. With British intellectuals the word is 'socialism'. Well, at least this is some advance. The mere apocalyptic event which produces the new society is not the fetish. Not, indeed, that the Russians didn't have 'socialism' too, among their sacred words, but it was more or less thought of in terms of that which would be produced by revolution. Here, at least, we have tended to concentrate on the actual nature of the 'good society'.

But what is 'socialism'? asked Conquest, jesting. And unlike Pilate stayed for an answer, without markedly better result. In its inspirational aspect the word 'socialism' conveys an economy without sin. In the old days, and partly through marxist jargon, the definition was easy – a society without capitalists. Unfortunately, since then a number of societies without capitalists have been created in various countries and it would take a word-fetishist of terrific obstinacy to maintain that these were indeed without sin.

For the trouble with word-fetishism when applied to an immensely complicated real situation, is that the word-man prefers to define reality in a few grand general terms, while reality goes on being as complex as ever and failing to respond. If 'capitalism' and 'socialism' were really the two legitimate terms for describing modern industrial societies, then under any definition which is not the merest mysticism the United States is not only more 'capitalist' than Russia, it is also (if socialism is definable as society controlling the economy) more 'socialist'. An intolerable situation.

It is the fetishism of abstract nouns which makes it intolerable – particularly ones which have gained a specially sacred status by beginning with capital letters. Of course, this applies not only in politics. In the arts too, the thing is to invent not the method, but the word. 'Action Painting', for example; or 'Concrete Poetry' – which is neither concrete nor poetry. But let me finish with a highly emotive word which has not yet got its capital letter: 'abortion'.

I was reading the other day a story by that remarkable science fiction writer, Philip Dick. We are set in a future in which legal wrangles have gone on for many years about the moment at which a foetus or baby becomes an independent human being. This has led – piecemeal – to a situation in which first of all the newborn child is abortable. After all, he is still a totally dependent entity. The mere fact of breathing has no ethical significance, being a simple physiological matter. And so on, and so on, till at the time Dick is writing of abortion can be carried out up to the age of fourteen, as the child is *still* not a totally independent human being. And so vehicles like the old dog-catcher trucks of the silent films go round the streets picking up boys and taking them to the pound for 'abortion'.

A fantasy? Yes. But 'revolution' led gradually to practically the same result, didn't it?

David Martin

A command of words

Some people tell me I've got what they call a 'command of words'. I'm not sure if its true but it's rather flattering and it makes me feel like a general. They say I summon words up with ease. Words jump to my attention and I marshal them sentence by sentence. I order them to appear and then I order them in lines and sequences. They obey the requirements of my argument. Looking at a blank sheet of paper I'm like a general looking at a map; the main gist is there, the supporting considerations waiting here, the main communication line just so. If the first line melts away I have a second line at hand.

I can even dress my words in enemy colours so that he welcomes them as allies. Then they shoot him down from behind. I know which of my words are traitors and I hold them under a tight chain of command. They are many-sided so they mustn't be allowed to change sides. I drill these ambiguous, traitorous words, cutting them down to size, making them perform certain specialised tasks. Or else I exploit their treason, altering their appearance till they create confusion all over the mental field. Then I bring up clean sharp words to cut through.

Naturally I keep fresh words in reserve. As the conventional words of my usual line get battle soiled I bring in others to do the same job. Even a good word like 'standards' can be crippled by enemy gas. Some words are contaminated by the company they keep. Our national 'stock' for example is wrecked by bad company and it wrecks you if you use it. 'Fascist' and 'reactionary' will fight for anybody: you don't want mercenaries on your side. 'Democracy' is a corrupt word. 'The people' is an expression to be left alone: it is the natural servant of the enemies of the people. The decent, serviceable word is just 'people'.

So logoi, words, serve the needs of logic and argument. They can be drilled in the logistics of contention. You don't win the battle of course, but you hold your ground. You keep, as they say, 'a command of words'.

Yet even the best generals lose some battles. Words fall out instead of standing to. Words fail me. It is all very well when I'm contending with words because that's the kind of military exercise in which words have been well schooled. Words have gone through the academies and pass out able to obey the requirements of argument. It's when I want them for more personal purposes that they go and leave me. I'm lost for words. Ask words for a personal favour and they die on your lips. Even the good upright words are caught in a quagmire of imprecision. You're stuck for words. They can't do what you ask because it is not just an exercise or a move in verbal chess but it's what you've seen with your own eyes. Words only come to attention for the things that every eye can see. They were born and shaped out of what people shared. If you ask them to speak for you about what only you have seen they fail you.

What happens then? I start to use words that say I've seen something I can't express. They are the common sentries which mark the frontiers of the inexpressible. They point across the frontier into a land which is no man's land but your own. And you know that everybody else is calling on these sentries standing at the margin of the articulate. They face towards a country of the mind to which you point but which lies beyond your command. Words like ecstasy, annihilation, apprehension, analogy, and shadow only infiltrate it. The frontier stays sealed. You can speak of darkness and light and shade on the other side but you can't convey the summer on the hill's shoulder or the unique familiar contour.

I make words my servants but for what I most want to say language binds me hand and foot. Words fail me. I've been relieved of my command.

Thee I love

I don't like 'you' but I do love 'thee'. I love 'thee'. Ich liebe dich. Je t'aime. Ego amo te. Do you like 'te'? I like 'te' and 'thee' because they are part of the language of religion and love. Admittedly, they're part of the traditional language of religion and love. 'With my body I *thee* worship.' Love and worship go together and so do the words which go with them.

Of course, if today I want to write a brand-new love poem to you I don't write it to 'thee'. 'Thee' or 'thou' would be artificial. A lover doesn't want someone who has been set in a glass case and embalmed in an outworn convention.

But there's place for convention. It's conventional to recite Shakespeare in his language not ours.

'Shall I compare thee to a summer's day?

Thou art more lovely and more temperate.'

Nobody is so stupid or so clever that they can attempt to refurbish Shakespeare in the language of today. Words, rhythm and verbal music are one and indivisible. Alter a word and you're convicted of blasphemy against perfection.

But what if you're talking to the one and indivisible God? Do you use the words of today or yesterday to speak of one who is the same yesterday, today and forever? Love of God is special. Religious language is not just a matter of my personal liking but reflects the way a company of men and women place themselves alongside generation after generation. For centuries people have recited together prose poems about divine love. These poems are full of simple things like cleansing water and the purifying fire, and such feelings as pleading and glorifying, sorrowing and rejoicing. People have said these words in the way they once heard tales and epics. The familiarity set their minds free. The rhythms and repetitions gave them quiet.

Nowadays it's all very different. The satisfying shapes and rhythms are gone and you don't know what to expect. Maybe you'll hear the old words, or a half-hearted translation or a whole-hearted translation. And usually the translations are very ill done. They're the work of ecclesiastical bureaucrats not of poets.

Take that old and simple declaration of divine love between priest and people.

'Dominus vobiscum. Et cum spirito tuo.'

Or, as the Prayer Book has it:

'The Lord be with you. And with thy Spirit.'

Clearly 'thy' was marked for destruction. But the real offence lay in 'spirit'. Perhaps people brought up in a scientific age might think that the priest had a spirit. They might easily see him as a man with a detachable spirit corked up in a bottle. So the ecclesiastics chased the 'spirit' out and produced this:

'The Lord be with you. And also with you.'

They had succeeded only in one thing: crippling the language of love. They got rid of the spirit and exorcised the beauty.

The old words are going unless we do something about it. 'They' – the commissions and committees – have decided against words we can love. The words of love and the love of the Word may pass away together. The really great words are to be stored in a museum and stumbled on accidentally by students of English literature. The old Calvinist at least had a good reason for breaking down the ranks of medieval statuary. The new Puritan is just a specialist in verbal whitewash. He obscures the images, obliterates the shapes, covers up the colours. He hopes people will forget what they've lost just as people forgot the mutilated stumps which had once been statues. We have even been offered a translation of the hymns. It has a splendid contemporary title: *Cantate Domino.*

D. J. Enright

Proverbial wisdom

There is a Dutch proverb which says: 'Proverbs are the daughters of daily experience'. In that case daily experience must vary considerably from day to day, since those daughters seem to spring from very different fathers. Quite often one proverb is blankly contradicted by another. 'Look before you leap' – yes, but what about 'He who hesitates is lost'? 'God help the poor, for the rich can help themselves' – yes, but also: 'God help the rich, the poor can beg'. 'A good tale is none the worse for being twice told' is barely reconcilable with 'A tale twice told is cabbage twice sold'. Two of the most quoted cancel themselves out: 'Many hands make light work' and 'Too many cooks spoil the broth'. Then, as we know, 'Absence makes the heart grow fonder' – but before you stake your love life or professional career on that sage counsel remember this: 'Out of sight, out of mind'. Incidentally, those who still treasure the human touch and distrust the mechanical will be glad to hear that when a highly sophisticated computer was set to translating English idioms into foreign tongues, 'Out of sight, out of mind' re-emerged in Japanese as 'Invisible, insane'. For a proverb to survive, for it to become a proverb, it needs to embody a considerable measure of proven truth, and the explanation of this mutual contradictoriness must lie in that wise remark of Dr Johnson's, in *Rasselas*, about inconsistencies: 'Inconsistencies cannot both be right, but, imputed to man, they may both be true'.

Then there is the cryptic class of proverbs, those which leave us baffled and uneasy, with the feeling that something sinister is being hinted at. For instance, 'An egg will be in three bellies in twenty-four hours' sounds obscurely frightening, and so does 'Everything hath an end, and a pudding hath two'. The saying that goes: 'He that hath a head of wax must not walk in the sun' causes us to feel our own heads in trepidation. The one that tells us 'A dog's nose and a maid's knees are always cold' gives us to think seriously about its intention, and so does 'You should never rub your eyes with your elbows' – there's something of the Zen *koan* in that one. 'A lisping lass is good to kiss': that may be true on the literal plane, but we wonder what profound metaphorical significance it is bringing to our attention. And since the saying 'All promises are either broken or kept' is on the face of it a truism, what esoteric and novel truth must surely be concealed beneath? At times one begins to suspect that a number of proverbial sayings had their origin in some ancient equivalent of the *New Statesman* Weekend Competition.

There is a Scottish proverb which has it that 'A white wall is a fool's paper'. Graffiti are more often than not the work of fools or worse, and I don't wish to encourage the recent tendency to pass them off as not merely another form of folk wisdom and wit but an art form comparable in its achievements to the writings of Shakespeare or Milton – though I can see a superficial resemblance to the genre of painting called by the Japanese 'shunga' (a nice euphemism, that: literally it means 'art in season'). I shall therefore quote only the two which stick in my mind. The first of these I found staring me in the face in a gents' urinal, and (I would venture) it strikes too sombre a chord to be called indecent: 'The future of England lies in your hands'. The second is well known, even hackneyed, but such is its resonance that I shall cite it all the same. 'God is dead: signed Nietzsche', with below it, in another hand, a second inscription: 'Nietzsche is dead: signed God'. We know that Nietzsche is dead and God may well have the last word after all.

I was hoping that this digression into the wisdom of the wall would take up the remainder of my time and thus furnish me with an honourable excuse for not mentioning a certain other proverbial saying. Alas it hasn't, and so I must. This one runs: 'Wise men make proverbs and fools repeat them'.

The art of blurbs

The writing of blurbs for book jackets or publishers' catalogues is a difficult art, and the results commonly please no-one, and certainly not the author of the book. Here is a specimen which at least possesses the putative virtues of accuracy, informativeness and modesty: 'We have little hesitation in claiming that this relatively new book by Mr X represents an advance on the author's previous one, which nonetheless received rather favourable mention in a leading provincial newspaper. The present book is well written, in a style which combines the gritty with the fluid. Not so much a novel as an extended documentary prose-poem, it is an account of good and evil in a contemporary setting and all of us, whether men or women. "The Spenser of Trollopes" is how the *Eriskay Reporter* has described Mr X . . . ' and so forth. Mind you, there is one class of persons who appreciate blurbs: the reviewers. Many a brilliantly mordant review owes more to the blurb than to the book, or to the reviewer.

Not long ago I found myself having to shorten a number of blurbs for an overcrowded list of forthcoming publications. From 250 words to 150, to 100, then to 50. Impossible though further cutting seemed each time, yet it proved not only possible but preferable as well: finally I arrived at an admirably economical description of the essence of the book. But then I had to go and put words back in. Readers aren't happy with essences, whether in blurbs or in books: it seems they need a generous emulsion of words in which their minds can float comfortably, they need a fair amount of verbal roughage, or of verbal smoothage. Many of the words don't get noticed at all, and if all that was offered were essence, then the essence might go unobserved. I know we were taught that in great writing every word is strictly necessary, and cannot be replaced by any other, and there is not a super-fluous syllable. I'm sure that is true. But I don't think I am talking about *great* writing – there is never very much of that on the scene at any one time. I don't think I am talking about great readers, either. Heaven help the poor publisher if he had to depend solely on great writers and great readers!

Some writers are not very good at reading their own writing, even. Recently I was studying a book by an academic, the theme of which was the symbolism of excretory processes in the works of Virginia Woolf: a new insight into this celebrated novelist, I should imagine, and one likely to show how highly 'relevant' she is. The scholar had been discussing a story entitled 'The Ladies' Lavatory', and went on in the next sentence to refer to a novel called *Flush*. As a matter of fact I did know that *Flush* was the name of a dog, but the associations evoked by the contiguity were such as to de-molish that suspension of disbelief so often required when reading academic exegesis.

Mistakes or insensitivities incurred by people writing in a language not their own is a different matter, not open to con-tempt or reproach. Sometimes they have a splendour of their own. I remember in the late 1940s being impressed by an Egyptian student's reference to 'this age of atomic pomp': it evoked a romantic image of nuclear reactors in the shape of great pyramids, with the sphinx brooding over them. A little later I realised that the confusion between 'p' and 'b' was at work, this being a distinction non-existent in Arabic – in fact we use the forms 'Pasha' and 'Basha' indifferently, since the original sound is somewhere in between. What the student actually had in mind was the atomic bomb.

But back to our blurbs. The dictionary tells us only that the word 'blurb' originated in American slang. My theory has it that the word is a skilful conflation of a number of other words, among them 'blur', 'bluff', 'blub', 'blush', 'bluster', 'burble', 'babble', 'burp' and 'blunder'. As I say, a difficult art.

Margaret Drabble

Confessions of a punster

I would like to make a defence of the pun. I know that there are some who think the pun the lowest form of wit, and who complain frequently to such newspapers as indulge themselves most lavishly in the form, but all I can say is that they cheer me up enormously.

I am in good company. Shakespeare was fond of puns too, even of bad ones. The good ones we can call ambiguities and thereby pardon them, but some of them, introduced at moments of high drama, are merely puns – as, for instance, Lady Macbeth's remark, when she plans to smear the faces of the sleeping grooms with blood – 'I'll gild the faces of the grooms withall, for it must seem their guilt'. Even at a moment like that, Shakespeare couldn't resist it, like a *Guardian* headline writer. But some of his puns are really so rich in their double meanings, so reverberating in their implications, that they make one wonder about the nature of language. My favourite is the pun on lying to and lying with, which he makes in the sonnets: 'Therefore I lie with her, and she with me. And in our faults by lies we flattered be'. Implying that only by mutual deceit can they make love at all, so untruthful are they with one another. 'When my love swears that she is made of truth, I will believe her, though I know she lies', the sonnet begins. And she lay with others, as well as with him. I find this pun so deeply satisfying that I would happily claim that it said something profound about the nature of sex and honesty and love, were it not for the fact that it can't as far as I know be translated into any other language. So it's only a piece of verbal dexterity, after all, rather than a double meaning of Jungian universality.

I like making puns myself, but some of them are so obscure that nobody ever notices them. I particularly like puns that depend on a knowledge of a word's original derivation. My favourite of my own is a phrase in which one of my characters describes his skill at card tricks. He describes it as 'a sinister dexterity'. To appreciate the full glory of this one must of course know that the character in question is left-handed, so he is describing the paradox of his own nature by calling it a left-handed right-handedness. I find that very satisfying, though I've never yet met anyone else who liked it, I have to admit. One could go on to discuss how sinister came to mean bad, wicked and suspicious, and why the left-handed, those of the bar sinister, have always been thought wicked, but I believe it would take a whole anthropological tract to do the subject justice, and somebody else has written it.

Occasionally one finds one has made puns by accident. There is one sentence I once wrote in which I still cannot decide whether I meant impunity or immunity or possibly both. When I was on a lecture tour recently a teacher pointed out to me that in the last sentence of *The Needle's Eye* I use the phrase 'weathered into identity' to mean 'weathered into selfness, particularity, individuality, true identity' when it could equally be taken to mean its exact opposite – that is, weathered into identical similarity. In context, this is a most disturbing unintentional pun.

But, all in all, I rejoice that such possibilities of double meaning exist. They rise out of a sense that meaning transcends words, and that plays on words are more than mere game. They reveal the natural accord of the universe, bringing together like and unlike, despite our efforts to differentiate. The pun does what Dr Johnson accused the metaphysical poets of doing – it yokes heterogeneous ideas by violence together, a device which distressed Dr Johnson, but which I find somehow reassuring.

The fiendish curse

I wonder how many thousands of English schoolgirls have
giggled themselves into hysteria and their schoolteachers
into despair over the moment when Tennyson declares:
> 'The curse is come upon me, cried
> The Lady of Shallott.'

What a joke, how impossible, what can Tennyson have been
thinking of, first of all to call the lady after a kind of onion,
and then to mention that shocking female secret, 'the curse'?
Thinking of this, and the impossibility of ever taking that
poem seriously in class, I reflected upon the extreme ugliness
of most of the words and phrases that describe the female
condition. The curse is bad enough – Carrington had her own
phrase for it and called it 'the fiend', but equally depressing
are those phrases for the curse's ending – menopause, change
of life, they are enough in themselves to frighten the middle-
aged into depression. There is a description of menstruation
in Simone de Beauvoir's *The Second Sex* that is so horrifying,
so depressing in detail and language, that one feels quite faint
after reading it – and yet, at the end of it, I found myself saying to myself 'But this is nonsense, this doesn't describe
what it is like at all, in no way is being female like that'.
Maybe I'm lucky, but I can't be the only lucky one. And anyway, why haven't some of the lucky ones amongst us been
able to invent a few more positive words, some more sym-
pathetic language? What have women been up to, all these
centuries, guiltily accepting their own uncleanliness, trund-
ling off to hospital to hear themselves described, at the age of
thirty-five, as an 'elderly prima gravida'.

Perhaps it is too late to create a more positive language
for menstruation. It will remain at best a bad joke, not fit for
serious discussion or elevated literature. But why? What
is there more undignified about the cycle of the body than
about the ebb and flow of the tides, the changing form of the
moon? Surely it would once have been possible to derive
some natural monthly symbols. It is fashionable to mock the

makers of contraceptive pills who recognise that women like to bleed even when sterile, but what is there wrong with bleeding? The fact that at least some of us are reassured by the sight of our own blood does mean that there is not that total universal hostility to the monthly experience that all the other evidence suggests. Too late to reinstate it, and don't think I'm not sorry for all those to whom it is indeed a fiend and a curse. But those of us who don't suffer should say a good word for it every now and then. If only there were a good word to say. But there isn't. There aren't any good words, in this area.

I came up against this shortage of female language most acutely when writing my novel *The Waterfall*, which is the most female of all my books, beginning with childbirth, travelling through sex, and ending up with a thrombic clot resulting from contraceptive pill-taking. Describing childbirth was all right; there are some good words. I don't object to labour, deliverance, travail – and there is something rather poetic about the phrase 'and then the waters broke' – much better than talk of ruptured membranes, anyway. Cord, after-birth, stitches, scars, breasts – all good, acceptable words. But as soon as one starts to describe visits to post-natal clinics one runs into trouble. I wanted to write a touching scene in the post-natal clinic, where my protagonist, waiting to be examined, realises that she is made whole again after the birth. Why not, after all? A significant moment in her emotional life, it would have been, and there wasn't any possible way of describing it. In the end I avoided it and allowed her, rather reluctantly, to sit there getting frightened again; – frightened, as she says, of the rubber fingers and the gynaecological rubber language. As she would have been. As most of us are. But how much better if she could have sat there in a different scene in a different book with different words, not frightened, but made whole. It's a book I can't write, an area I abandon. But reluctantly, reluctantly.

Dear sib

It is fashionable these days to sneer at the jargon of sociology and one would indeed be hard pushed to find a defence for such nouns as 'problematic' and 'imageability' or for such strange desires as 'N.Ach' and 'N.Aff'. But other words come quite unnecessarily under fire. Take for instance the word 'sibling'. Sibling is in my view one of the most useful and attractive of recent coinages; it saves many meaningless verbal complexities; it's sexually non-discriminatory; it adds elegance to a sentence. I put this point of view to a friend recently and he said 'Oh but it's such an ugly word'. Well, is it? Of course it isn't. It is a pleasant word, sweet, affectionate, of ancient root, an ancient root with a new end. 'Sib' is an old term for relative, like 'coz'; one imagines it was not very precise. 'Dear sib' one can imagine a member of a family saying to another not quite specified blood relation. And the diminutive 'sibling' like darling sounds to me both charming and familial. It has a more specific meaning than 'sib' and a key to its utility is the number of times one finds oneself using or reading it in correct context in non-sociological prose. Society needed a word for 'sibling' and in 1897 it sensibly created one.

There are other words that society or sociology ought to coin, and no doubt will, and particularly in this vexed area of kinship. As our family and kinship patterns change so we create needs for new words of relationship. The word 'sibling' and its popularity must be associated with the increase in the number of children from complex rather than monogamous marriage patterns, for the term embraces half-brothers and half-sisters as well as full ones and how pleasantly the word embrace fits the context here.

There was an article in The *Guardian* some time ago about the need for a new word to replace 'stepmother', for 'stepmother' has such wicked fairy-tale connotations and doubtless in the old days of property battles there were plenty of wicked stepmothers. Nowadays one knows mainly benevolent ones, kindly accommodating small troops of infants from their husbands' past while their husbands' first wives divert themselves elsewhere. Divorce has added some strange sounds to kinship words. I met a man in the post office last week trying, he said, to choose an appropriate birthday card for his ex-stepmother, a complex relationship there and one that needs another more natural term to embrace it and other such relationships.

Kinship words have always presented delicate problems. Who has not suffered hesitation over choosing a form of address for his mother-in-law. By surname? By first name? As mother, as ma, as mama? Stepmothers are still relatively rare but mothers-in-law abound. Perhaps it's more delicate not to distinguish between them like the French and Charles Dickens in *Pickwick Papers*.

And there are many other tricky areas. What about the word 'boyfriend' or 'mistress' or 'lover'? As we know the word 'lover' used to indicate friendship without a specific sexual context but it isn't really on now to introduce a friend as 'a lover'. But I cannot be the only person to wince with embarrassment when I hear a forty-five-year-old present another forty-five-year-old with the phrase 'and this is my boyfriend'. On the other hand I knew somebody who went around saying proudly 'and this is my man' and found herself being accused of being an unliberated sexist. Again there may be those who get a thrill out of being described as X's 'mistress' when really all they are doing is living respectably with X in sin.

There are many pitfalls in language particularly in areas of moral confusion and social change. Perhaps it's not surprising that we are diffident and apologetic about our new society and that our language reflects this uncertainty. But relationships need words and words help to reinforce relationships and those who have confidence ought to be able to find the words.

Kenneth Tynan

Cultural outsiders

John Higgins, of whom you are very unlikely to have heard, was born in or around 1545. I first – and last – came across him in C. S. Lewis's history of English literature in the sixteenth century. Higgins was a minor – or rather minimal – playwright and in one of his plays there appears a ghost who says:

'I pray thee, Higgins, take in hand thy pen . . . '

Now that sounds to us wrong and so does this – Wordsworth beginning a sonnet with the ringing lines:

'Jones! as from Calais southward you and I
Went pacing side by side . . . '

But nobody laughed. And they took him equally seriously when he opened another poem thus:

'Spade, with which Wilkinson hath tilled
his lands . . . '

Yet to us the use of such prosaic names as Higgins, Jones and Wilkinson in a poetic context sounds bizarre. Why is this?

The first clue I have to offer is that not all surnames are equally funny. We don't feel disposed to giggle when Milton addresses his contemporaries in lines like: 'Fairfax, whose name in arms through Europe rings', or 'Lawrence, of virtuous father virtuous son . . . '

These are names that have about them a brave and chivalric ring – a touch of class. We don't feel the same deference –

the same sense that the person invoked is a fit subject for eulogy – when Shelley writes that:

'. . . Wit and sense,
Virtue and human knowledge . . .
Are all combined in Horace Smith'.

My next clue is that drab names nowadays seem hilarious only in certain kinds of poetry. We don't object to them in dialect verse or folk poetry. Nothing seems wrong when Burns, for instance, pays tribute to 'John Anderson, my Jo', any more than it does when an American folk singer hymns the virtues of a working-class hero called 'John Henry'.

The third clue has to do with chronology. It's clear that Wordsworth's and Shelley's readers took Jones, Wilkinson and Horace Smith in their stride. It's only later that poets begin to shun these vulgar surnames: we don't find them in Tennyson or Browning. The inference must be that something happened in the early part of the nineteenth century to exclude proletarian names from serious poetry.

What happened was the industrial revolution, and the sudden, enormous growth of an industrial working class. The overwhelming majority of poets and readers of poetry had come from the middle classes. Almost overnight, names like Jones and Smith acquired associations that simply couldn't be assimilated into the world of respectable art. Poetry, in a word, became class-conscious. Readers and writers alike became infected with the taint of snobbism.

Poetry turned in on itself, and away from the new and squalid world of industry, technology and dark satanic mills. Where Wordsworth could still feel he was addressing a whole nation, from the peasantry up to the peerage, later poets – consciously or unconsciously – addressed only their own class. And, more especially, a cultured minority within it. And to have brought Jones, Robinson and Brown into that world would have been like bringing mud on your boots into the drawing-room. They would have been clumsy and potentially dangerous intruders.

When we laugh at their names in the poetry of the past, we are defining ourselves in a way that we should lament, for it does us little credit. We are ratifying and perpetuating a split that took place in English culture and has never been wholly healed. And this is true even in the work of the socialist poets of the 1930s. Auden and MacNeice may have sympathised with the aspirations of Jones, Robinson and Brown, but they could somehow never bring themselves to use these sordid surnames in poetry. Jones, Robinson and Brown remained – and remain still – cultural outsiders. And poetry became what, with few exceptions, it still is: the form in which the middle class enshrines its nostalgia and ennobles its anxieties.

Man, I dropped my eggs

We're constantly being reminded that language is a living organism and that it needs regular blood transfusions of colloquialism and slang if it's to keep alive and alert. But there is a special difficulty connected with slang, and that is the matter of actually *using* it. By which I mean using it without sounding phony, out of character or downright idiotic.

In England, far more than in the United States, we expect a person's speech habits to be all of a piece with his age and his class. If he uses slang that we associate with a different age group or class, we tend to raise our eyebrows or even to titter. One of the mainstays of English comedy is a working-class comic putting on a posh accent and using upper-class words – as anyone who saw the great Sid Field will confirm. When he said 'And how are you? Reasonably well, I hope?', it was funny simply because those words and that accent did not belong in that mouth. Comedy that's based on verbal incongruity is nearly always comedy based on class distinctions.

But the problem I want to examine has to do with age rather than class. I have a theory that human beings can be judged by the nature and quality of the slang that they use. For example, I don't think any Englishman feels really at home when using slang expressions that came into vogue after he was approximately forty years old. In my own case,

I feel at ease with words and phrases like 'cool it' in the sense of 'take it easy', 'pad' in the sense of 'apartment', and 'bread' in the sense of 'cash'. I can also use 'far out' without too much effort, because all these expressions come from American jazz, and I am a child of the jazz age, or at least of the Parlophone Rhythm Series of the 1930s. And I never had any trouble with 'put down' in the sense of 'humiliate' or of 'discomfit', because, like so much slang, it is a revival of a dormant Elizabethan usage. When Beatrice makes a fool of Benedick in *Much Ado About Nothing*, Don Pedro says: 'You have put him down, lady, you have put him down'. I can just about manage to say: 'I freaked', in the sense of 'I was thrown into confusion or panic'; but I cannot utter the phrase 'Right on!' to save my life; and there's no way in which I could be persuaded to say: 'No way'.

This is partly because I would sound as if I were trying to be trendy – that's another word I hate, though for different reasons – but also because I would feel like mutton dressed up as lamb; as if I were using words as magical rejuvenators, instant passports to eternal youth. I also try to avoid the slang that was current amongst adults during my childhood, be-cause it would date me – so I shun words like 'ripping' and 'tophole'. We are all caught in the same trap. To use one's parents' slang indicates a too conservative cast of mind: but to use one's children's slang is Peter Panish. The only solu-tion, I think, is that we should confine ourselves to the slang that was used by our own age-group between our twentieth and fortieth years – ie the period of our first maturity.

On the other hand, I think everyone should attempt to in-troduce at least one new slang phrase during his lifetime. A couple of years ago I began to get irritated by hipster phrases expressive of stunned admiration, such as 'I flipped my wig' or 'I blew my mind'. So I decided to invent one for my own use. It derived from a friendly competition between two Flor-entine artists – Donatello and Brunelleschi – to see who could design the best sculpture of the crucifixion. One day Donatello went out to buy some eggs for lunch. On the way home he called in at Brunelleschi's studio and as soon as he entered he saw his rival's crucifix, which so impressed him that he let his eggs fall to the floor. And so whenever I'm describing to a hippie assembly some event of startling beauty, I generally say: 'Man, I dropped my eggs!' Nine times out of ten they pretend to know what I mean, which I find extremely satisfying.

I also think we are entitled to use the slang of other ethnic groups whenever we can get away with it. When language erects racial barriers, it withers and dies. For people like myself, who work in and around show business, it is natural to borrow from Jewish slang, since – in the United States anyway – show business was virtually created by, and is still enormously dependent on, Jewish talent. Hence I can happily use such vivid and vicacious words as 'cockamamie', meaning 'far-fetched and ridiculous', 'schlock', meaning 'cheap or phony merchandise', 'dreck', meaning 'human excrement', and 'meshuggah', meaning 'crazy'. And above all, there is the indispensable word 'chutzpah', which means 'nerve, cheek or presumption'. On trips to New York, I sometimes have the 'chutzpah' to consider myself an honorary Jew.

Which reminds me, finally, of an unforgettable pun I once committed. I was talking to a great Shakespearian actor and I asked him how it came about that there were no Jewish actors in his company. He thought for a moment and then said that, outside *The Merchant of Venice*, there were no Jewish parts in the whole of Shakespeare. 'Nonsense', I said, thinking of *Henry IV, Part One*. 'What about Chutzpah?'

The right headline

One of the things that worries me about journalists is the way in which they use skilful verbal techniques to blur the all-important dividing line between fact, which belongs in the news pages, and comment, which belongs in the editorial section. In American or French newspapers, this distinction is always observed. You can attack a politician editorially, but in the news department you confine yourself to a strictly neutral account of his words and deeds.

In England, on the other hand, biased and emotive language is constantly invading news stories and headlines. And because the great majority of newspapers are owned by people of Tory inclination, the bias and the emotion tend to be anti-socialist. If the leader of a Left-wing union makes a powerful speech, it will be described as 'belligerent' or 'strident', and he will be accused of 'ranting'. Whenever the head of a communist or a socialist country makes a speech, he is said to 'bluster' – or, if he is in a conciliatory mood, to 'wheedle'. Mr Khrushchev, whatever he said, was invariably described as 'blustering'.

By contrast, conservative leaders appear in the papers as people who 'issue grave warnings' or 'spell out dangers'. It is always the workers who are 'threatening to bring the country to a standstill' because they are demanding too much money; it is never the management who are responsible, for having offered too little. When people take to the streets to protest against someone of whom the newspaper owners approve, they are described as 'a howling mob'. But when it's someone of whom the proprietors disapprove, the 'howling mob' turns into 'a demonstration of profound public feeling'.

In 1974, *The Times* ran a headline that read: 'Loyal Rolls Royce Worker Fined'. It turned out, when you read the item, that the man in question had been fined by his union for disobeying a strike order. He had thus been *disloyal* to his union. *The Times* took it for granted that a worker's loyalty automatically belonged to his employer.

In recent years the great spawning-ground of emotively biased reportage has centred on the career of Antony Wedgwood Benn. If a Tory became chairman of a party committee, we would read that he'd been 'appointed' to the post. When someone like Mr Benn is elected to a similar position, the headline says 'Benn Seizes New Job' – as if he had done it by force. When the Industry Bill was published the *Daily Mail* published a characteristic headline: 'Benn's Great Grab Plan'. Verbs implying theft, with overtones of violence, are frequently employed when the sanctity of private property is in question. The attitudes expressed in this kind of usage get absorbed into our intellectual bloodstream. They simply reflect the convictions of the small group of people who own and control our press. So whenever we find in a news item a word that implies a value judgement, we are in the presence of corrupt journalism.

The same applies to the way our newspapers report crime. A fine illustration came up when Lord Lucan was accused of the murder of his children's nanny. When the police announced that they were seeking to arrest the vagabond peer, one newspaper reported that many of Lord Lucan's friends were, as the journalist put it, 'dedicated men' who would not hesitate to shelter him. But what if the wanted man had been not Lord Lucan, but Harry Noakes of Bermondsey? Harry's friends would not have been called 'dedicated men': they would have been 'underworld cronies'. Some reports expressed fears that, rather than face trial, Lord Lucan might have committed suicide, in order 'to avoid causing distress to his children'. I can't imagine anyone attributing such laudable motives to Harry Noakes.

Most revealing of all was the language used by television newscasters reporting the case. 'Lord Lucan is *still missing*'. I have no doubt how they would have described the case of Harry Noakes, in similar circumstances. 'Harry Noakes', they would have said, 'is still on the run'.

R. W. Burchfield

Appearing like pustules

There are six main meanings of the word 'eruption' in the *Oxford English Dictionary*, most of them being specialised applications of the basic sense 'a bursting forth' or 'a breaking out'. Somewhat surprisingly the word was not associated with volcanoes until 1740 and the earliest recorded occurrences are to do with 'pustules' (in a fifteenth-century treatise on surgery), with 'springs out of the mountains', and with 'a sudden breaking out of mirth'. Whereas most new words enter the language quietly, others continue to appear like pustules, or like springs out of the mountains, or like a sudden breaking out of mirth. Such 'eruptions' place lexicographers in a quandary because the normal processes of classification and definition tend to be overwhelmed by the sheer quantity of the new arrivals.

The problem isn't new. In the Anglo-Saxon period the English language was full of words with certain prefixes and suffixes. For example, anyone compiling a glossary of Anglo-Saxon words knows how difficult it is to deal with all the words beginning with the lightly stressed prefix 'ge-'. In the later medieval period the prefix 'be-' tended to become ubiquitous and was even added to loanwords from the romance languages – for example the words 'becalm' and 'besiege'. Later again all kinds of problems were posed by the bursting forth of words with initial 'in-' or 'en-.' Nearly every word of long standing in the language, which is formed with 'en-' has at some period been written also with 'in-'. Considerable confusion results when pairs of words like 'enable' and 'inable', 'enaction' and 'inaction', and so on, turn up in works of the Renaissance period, and the sense can often only be determined by the context. To meet such challenges the compilers of glossaries adopted various ruses: among them cross-referencing, the provision of explanatory notes at the head of glossaries, and the ignoring of awkward language features.

Some people may imagine that in our own age new words would fit into slots that were fashioned for them decades or even centuries ago. But this is far from the case.

Of twentieth-century 'eruptions' the pustules include formations with the final element 'person', as in 'chairperson', 'spokesperson', and even 'gentlepersons'. Those like 'springs out of a mountain' include modern words with final '-in', for example 'teach-in' (modelled on earlier 'stay-in' and 'sit-in'), though of course the multiplication of such words can become tiresome – 'be-in', 'love-in', 'preach-in', and all the rest of them. And as for those like a 'sudden breaking out of mirth' these include words ending in '-nik' like 'beatnik', 'no-good-nik', and 'peacenik'.

Such comparatively small classes of words, however, though often tedious to deal with in dictionaries, don't pose insuperable problems. Very few of them are presented as main entries – only words as common as 'beatnik' and 'teach-in' of those I've just mentioned. The remainder are grouped in a kind of nest in the form of an entry for the terminal element itself, that is under '-in', '-nik', and '-person'.

But the problems are intensified enormously when a prefix such as 'non-' erupts like a volcano as it has done in the present century. The material for 'non-' in the new *Supplement to the Oxford English Dictionary* looks like breaking all records for the amount of space consumed by a single group of words. The obvious formations of 'non-' plus adjectives alone, like 'non-academic', exceed 400 in number, not to speak of 'non-' plus noun like 'non-cooperation', 'non-' plus noun used attributively like 'non-aggression pact', triple-membered phrases like 'non-habit-forming', and more recent phrases like 'non-iron', 'non-skid', and 'non-stick', where 'non-'

means 'not needing to be treated in a specified way' or 'not behaving in a specified way'. There is also Ian Gilmour's coinage 'non-event'.

This eruption has left us reeling. There were two minor comforts: whereas under 'anti-' we had to allow for a number of 'anti-anti' items like 'anti-anti-missile' it was a relief to find that our extensive files contained no information about any 'non-non' items. And the Renaissance habit of adding 'non-' to verbs, as to 'non-act', to 'non-preach', has not been revived in the present century. That is something I certainly non-regret!

A rare kicksy-wicksy

I heard recently that the allied soldiers in Gallipoli in 1915 put up a notice which read: 'The Turkish artillery is requested to refrain from wasting ammunition whilst our meals are being served.'

I must say that I sometimes wish that the general public would refrain from forming new words while we deal with those that have come into English since the *Oxford English Dictionary* was completed in 1928.

Many of the new words are well formed and are pleasant to use and to define. But there are some classes of new words, that give me more than usual pleasure; among them words that are extremely rare.

Degrees of rareness are often hard to establish but when only one instance of the use of a word was known to the editors of the *Oxford English Dictionary* they labelled it *rare*[1]. Such words are scattered throughout the dictionary and vary greatly in type and meaning. Some are humorous, like 'kicksy-wicksy', defined as 'a jocular or ludicrous term for a wife'. It occurs in Shakespeare's *All's Well that Ends Well*:

'He weares his honor in a box unseene
That hugges his kicksie-wicksie at home.'

Some are temporary and now obsolete variants, such as the word 'inadulterate' used by Herrick to mean 'unadulterated'. Some *rare*⁻¹ words are learned formations, such as 'sphairistic' meaning 'lawn-tennis-playing' (from the Greek σφαιριστική 'playing at ball').

There is in fact an even rarer species of word, labelled *rare*⁻⁰ in the *Oxford English Dictionary*. These are words that are recorded only in older dictionaries and are not traced in any literary source. In this category are such words as 'impigrity' meaning 'quickness', recorded in at least four dictionaries before Dr Johnson's and presumably lurking unnoticed in some Renaissance writer's work; and then there's 'implumous' meaning 'without feathers', listed by Johnson, and in later dictionaries, but unsupported by literary examples.

One of the powers that lexicographers have is to admit or omit words that in the nature of things lie at the borderline of acceptance. The central core of words in a dictionary is uncontested but at the edges a line must be drawn somewhere. This peripheral area is made up of dialect and slang words, specialised technical and scientific vocabulary, foreign loanwords, and so on.

Even in such a large dictionary as the *Oxford English Dictionary* the imperatives of space and time force us to narrow the choice to those *rare*⁻¹ words that occur in the major writers of the period being treated, and even then only the items that prove to be editable, excluding, for example, puns, malapropisms, and other forms of word-play.

Bearing this in mind, what kind of modern words stand in this special category of *rare*⁻¹ in the *Supplement to the Oxford English Dictionary*? Let me give an example. It occurs in a letter that James Joyce wrote to the artist Frank Budgen in October 1920. It dealt partly with the derivation of the word 'syphilis' and Joyce refers to 'the cerebral *impotentising* drink of chastity'. 'Impotentising' has turned up nowhere else and will be labelled *rare*⁻¹ in the second volume of the Supplement.

These *rare*⁻¹ words are in fact not very numerous: their

value lies in the light they cast on the inventive powers of the writers concerned. Samuel Beckett occasionally uses such rare words, for example: 'nucleant'. And the class could be further illustrated by such words as 'nibcocked' in Dylan Thomas, 'inoperancy' in T. S. Eliot, and 'neotene' in a poem by W. H. Auden.

There is a related process of some interest – the revival in modern times of words that are marked *obsolete rare*[1] in the dictionary. Through this means Dr Johnson's 'unaccountable muskin' makes its way into James Joyce's *Ulysses*. And in a more trivial area the word 'nippily', recorded in the *Oxford English Dictionary* only once, in 1650, now appears daily in motoring contexts like: 'The Fiat handles nippily, with good roadholding'. Joyce's 'muskin' is a deliberate adoption of a disused word; but 'nippily' is the kind of word that lies ready for use at any time and needs but a small spark to set it going again.

The new explorers

At a conference in Florence in 1971 I showed a galley-proof of our entry for the word 'enzyme' to the editor in chief of the *Trésor de la Langue Française*, and asked him in what way his forthcoming entry for the corresponding French word would differ from ours. I was rather pleased with our entry: 'enzyme' had two senses, the obvious biochemical one, and one from a nineteenth-century theological work, and each sense was illustrated by precisely dated examples in the usual way. 'No comparison is possible,' he replied, 'because there won't be an entry in the *Trésor*. It is too technical for us.' The more we talked the more obvious it became that the strategy of this great multi-volume French dictionary differed in quite fundamental respects from our own. Technical and scientific terms were to be severely curtailed, as was slang. And really obscene terms and also overseas forms of French were to be totally excluded.

In the British tradition we have to go back more than 200 years to find the same kind of exclusions forming part of the grand strategy. Dr Johnson left out the coarse words that had appeared freely in dictionaries issued before his time, and he held the normal eighteenth-century contemptuous view of low words like 'cut' and 'leg'. As for technical terms, they simply couldn't be admitted because, he said, 'I could not visit caverns to learn the miner's language, nor take a voyage to perfect my skill in the dialect of navigation.'

Step by step the attitudes changed in this country and in the robust atmosphere of the Victorian age we find Dr Murray, the editor of the *Oxford English Dictionary*, declaring that he 'made incursions into nearly all the sciences' while he was a young teacher in Scotland. He also said that he had 'a mania for learning languages'. And so the strategy changed and the *Oxford English Dictionary* set new standards in expansionism and grandeur.

In the twentieth century we are taking Dr Murray's strategy to its logical conclusion. Vast new English dictionaries of special periods such as Middle English and special areas such as American English have been completed or are in progress, and all of them are recognisably based upon the British strategy rather than the French one. The *Supplement to the Oxford English Dictionary* is doing the same. We are treating the English of all English-speaking regions. Nabokov and Salinger are quoted as freely as Graham Greene and Anthony Powell, and it is the same with Canadian, Australian, Indian, West Indian, and South African writers. We have ventured into areas unexplored by Dr Johnson and Dr Murray, and excluded on principle by the compilers of the French dictionaries. For example, our second volume will contain many of the words used by American blacks. As each new wave of vocabulary advances we advance towards it. Now we are exploring the vocabulary of the oil-rigs. It was startling to find that the word 'oil-rig' itself is not in the *Oxford English Dictionary*, and that a 'rig' is defined merely as 'an apparatus for well-sinking'. The first oil-drills began their work in the 1850s more or less at the time of the gold rushes. But whereas the vocabulary of the gold-rush period is firmly planted in the English language, only now, as the North Sea exploration continues, are such words as 'stinger' and 'tool-pusher', 'drillship' and 'saturation dive' swiftly moving into the vocabulary of the British Isles. It is exciting to be able to capture these words and record their history and their continuing use as one more century of our language moves towards its close.

Cardew Robinson

A touch of class

On no less than four occasions in the past week I've bumped into friends each of whom, had I taken his words literally, I would have suspected of trying to convince me that he combined great wealth with the living habits of an old-time monarch.

The first one had a swollen face. When I asked him what was wrong, he muttered, as well he could, 'a shocking session with *my* dentist'. A day later I rang another friend to ask if he wanted a round of golf with me. 'Sorry old man', he said, 'appointment with *my* hairdresser'. *My* hairdresser indeed! I wandered disconsolately into the club and saw another member, one of the older ones. I was about to ask him for a game, (I'll play with anybody when I'm pushed) when he got off his stool and began to shuffle towards the door. He was bent like an old question mark. I thought 'he'll never play this morning, if ever!' I wasn't at all surprised when he groaned, 'It's the back. Off to see *my* osteopath'. The fourth man to enjoy apparently exclusive service told me he was just off to see what he called '*my* tailor'. He added 'I have a little man in Aldgate you know'.

I had a quick mental picture of four practitioners: dentist, osteopath, hairdresser and tailor, each awaiting the arrival of his lord and master.

It seems to me that people who use the possessive pronoun

in this way, usually do so in an accent which used to be called 'posh', later 'public school', and later still, either 'cut glass' or 'toffee-nosed'. Its users are nearly always in the occupational group broadly classified as 'white-collar workers' and most of them are 'executive types'. I have yet to hear a milkman, lorry driver, or labourer (either farm or council) refer to '*my* doctor'. 'I had to go to *the* doctor last week', that's what they'd say, and then they might add an interesting twist, 'Shocking pain in *me* back'. With a cockney milkman it's 'to *the* doctor with *my* back'. To golf club man it's 'to *my* osteopath with *the* back'. Yet the sort of chap who says '*my* osteopath' but '*the* back' usually runs down to Hove in *the* car, while the milkman would probably tell you that 'I went down to Southend in *my* car'. It would almost seem that the executive or white-collar class feels that even in socialist Britain it still owns in some way, the people who serve it; its medicos and its tailors and the rest; while the artisan class only gets possessive about its things.

This verbal distinction even continues to crop up occasionally in matrimony. The golf club man will invite you to 'Meet *the* wife', or '*the* better half'. The milkman will, more often than not, introduce you to '*my* wife' or talk about '*my* old woman'.

Can we deduce from this, that as we ascend the social scale, the spouse is thought of more as an object to be possessed, and less of a personal servant? Is the milkman really feeling possessive about Mrs Milkman when he uses the word '*my*'? Is Golf Club Man really being matrimonially egalitarian, or just ungallantly off-hand when he says '*the*'? Even these verbal class differences aren't watertight. Take the law under which we are all supposed to be equal. Golf Club Man almost invariably refers to '*my* solicitor', while *your* milkman won't even go to *the* solicitor. It's 'I'll have to see *a* solicitor'. In other words any old solicitor, picked out at random from the yellow pages, on the rare occasions that he is forced to seek one out.

So when it comes to people who supply a service there would seem to be a hierarchy among the people who employ that service, made up of the users of 'my', 'the', and rather timidly, 'a'.

Further thoughts upon the full social significance of all this must wait for the moment, as I have to get out *the* car, to drive with *my* old woman, to *a* solicitor. You will no doubt judge correctly that I shall be driving in the middle of the road!

Sheer savage music

Whenever I played cowboys and Indians as a boy, I always wanted to be an Indian. I'm still obsessed by the Red Indian and there are probably several reasons for this. It is partly sympathy for the under-dog; and partly a case of arrested romanticism. The Indians were so wonderfully picturesque in their costume and in their way of life. Their fate was tragic, their defence against overwhelmingly superior forces so heroic.

Yet one of the outstanding reasons for the abiding appeal was the mass of wonderful words associated with the American Indian. Just think of a few: tomahawk, tepee, scalp-lock, moccasin, squaw, pemmican, Mannito – the great spirit. At once you are back, not only in your own youth, but in the youth of the New World itself, among prairies and pine forests where the only air pollution was the minimal amount caused by the crisply scented wood fires.

Although they never exceeded half a million, the Indians were subdivided into so many tribes that, even now after years of interest and study, I occasionally come across one that is new to me. And those names! Even now, years after the last scalp was lifted, and the last homestead burned, the name Comanche is still a spine-tingler. And Apache! So synonymous with ruthless ferocity that it was transported to Europe to be shared with the savages of the Paris underworld. There were Sioux, Cheyenne, Winnebago, Potawatomi, the six nations of the Iroquois, Seneca, Mohawk, Cayuga, Oneida, Onondaga, Tuscarora. Sheer savage music. And those

French tribal names: Gros Ventres, Nez Perces. There were the Blackfeet (so-called from their dark moccasins). Shoshone, the snake Indians. And the five South Eastern tribes who became known as the civilised tribes: namely the Cherokees, Choctaws, Chickasaws and Creeks. Plus the Seminoles, who broke away from the Creeks, and were called outcasts by them, but remain the only tribe never conquered by the white man. This was partly due to the impenetrability of the superbly named Everglades of Florida whence they retreated between forays, and partly because of the military skill of their chief, Osceola. His is one of the names which in themselves sound like war cries. As do those of so many other chiefs like Geronimo, Cochise, Tecumseh. One Apache leader sounded like a Roman Emperor, Magnus Colaradus. Then there were the beautiful descriptive names: Red Cloud, Little Wolf, Rain-in-the-Face, Black Hawk, Yellow Hand, Crazy Horse. How much more attractive than our own Smiths, Jones, and of course, Robinsons! The nearest we ever get to Sitting Bull is Ramsbottom!

This diversity of tongue and tribe helped to make the Indians so fascinating to people like us. But it was partly responsible for their final defeat coming earlier than it might have done had they ever really managed to combine against their common enemy. Alas age old enmity was too deep-rooted between tribes such as the Huron and Iroquois; between Cree and Blackfeet, even to be buried in the cause of survival. A few attempts were made at a Grand Alliance; notably by Pontiac and Sitting Bull. But after Sitting Bull thrashed the prosaically named George Custer at Little Big Horn, the Indians experienced the final outrage at Wounded Knee. How sadly apt was the name of the location of that last red versus white encounter, for the wound was to prove fatal. Incidentally what a bit of verbal double standard it was which described the battle of the Little Big Horn as a massacre and the massacre of Wounded Knee as a battle.

As an Indianophile, I am grateful that Columbus thought he had landed in India and named the original native Americans accordingly. He could easily have been even more hazy as to his whereabouts with catastrophic verbal and nominal consequences. I can't for one moment imagine that I would have been equally thrilled in my youth and evermore by the tales of pony express riders making good their escape although pursued by painted, feathered bands of Red Chinese.

A multitude of animal-eaters

You don't have to be a dedicated animal lover to recognise the fact that over the years man has given the animal kingdom a pretty rough time, and is still doing so. We have chased them, shot them, trapped them, harpooned them, imprisoned them, stuffed them, and of course, eaten them. Have we eaten them! I remember hearing an American comedy record on which a lady starts to sing a beautiful song in a voice of great sweetness; suddenly as I was being carried away with the song a harsh American voice broke in. 'Lovely isn't she; spiritual you could say; unworldly. Well, it may interest you to know that so far in her life this unworldly young lady has consumed the equivalent of 124 bullocks, 205 sheep, 318 chickens, 300 pigs, to say nothing of thousands and thousands of fishes.' I'm not certain that I have remembered the figures correctly and realise that they were only a very rough approximation, but even so multiply these figures by the number of meat-eaters in the world and you'll get some idea of the massive slaughter that goes on for the sake of our sustenance, quite apart from that occasioned by vanity, cruelty, or cruelty masquerading as sport. Yet when the occasional animal reverses the process he is regarded with horror. A word like 'man-eater' drips with outraged disgust, yet man seldom if ever refers to himself as an 'animal-eater'! A meat-eater or carnivore, yes, but this is rather euphemistic and slightly begs the question.

One of my more vivid imaginings, usually after a large steak dinner, is of some kind of terrestial War Crimes Commission, where man is in the dock being judged by a jury consisting of a fox, a beaver, a pheasant, a whale, a trout, a hare, a seal, a stag, a rabbit, a pig, a sheep, and a bull. I feel that it would go hard for him. The only animals likely to appear as witnesses for the defence would be the dog, for certain, maybe the cat, and possibly the horse.

Many men, of course, have sought to redress the balance, and among them are the word makers responsible for collective nouns. In this respect man comes off second best. Collections of humans are referred to by words like 'crowd', or 'multitude', both of which convey an impression of discomfort, even if they are not as unpleasant as 'mob' or 'rabble' with all their nasty implications. 'Tribe' usually means a collection of backward natives or unwashed children. 'Gang' speaks, unspeakably, for itself. So does 'posse' with its visions of lynchings.

There is hardly a kind word to be said for a gathering of human beings even if they happen to be nice; even 'assemblage' sounds stuffy. In contrast consider some of the picturesque terminology used to describe groups of animals, the otherwise under-privileged inhabitants of our planet. Top of the list must come 'pride' which magnificently describes a group of lions. A 'mischief' of monkeys is almost too delightful to be true. And what about a 'charm' of finches? That graceful compliment pays back a little bit of the debt incurred by the bird-cagers. The word 'flush' suggests that mallards may possess unsuspected sensitivity. I like a 'sounder' of swine and a 'gaggle' of geese; onomatopoeia at its best that last one. Only the poor old fox comes out of this less than well: the age old enmity between Reynard and man seems to be perpetuated in our choice of 'skulk' for him – although it does conjure up a vivid picture. 'Herd' sounds faintly derogatory; but then 'flock' is surely a polite word when it is applied to starlings who often behave much more like a 'rabble'. 'School' is pleasant enough, though when one remembers the behaviour of porpoises, it would seem that theirs was perpetually on holiday.

These vivid words show up the drabness of the human collective nouns. Perhaps the time has come for innovation; can't we invent new words for groups of people? How about an 'aggravation' of hooligans, a 'protest' of students, a 'natter' of disc jockeys, a 'pain' of dentists, a 'squeeze' of tax collectors, and a 'titter' of comedians? How about some local ones: a 'drench' of Mancunians perhaps, or a 'cider' of West Countrymen?

Many individuals in any of the groups could no doubt claim justly that they were not at all like the description implied by the collective noun. But here too animals are different. In any collection of animals the characteristics of the pack, flock, or pride, are usually those of each individual in it. This may be one of the more hopeful things that raises man above the animals!

Ian Robinson

Alas it's ironic

Every word and every sentence can be used ironically. There is no sentence in which either the words or some principle of organisation will guarantee that they are being used not ironically but 'straight'. On the other hand it is peculiarly true of our age that many words can *only* be used ironically; the most obvious examples are words which in former ages could be used to express a deep belief or emotion that has now somehow evaporated, leaving to our cynical times only a necessary or routine sneer.

'Honour' can perhaps just about still be used straight, 'noble' only very doubtfully, 'gentleman' and 'lady' never. In the fourteenth century people actually exclaimed 'Alas!' when they wanted to express their sadness. When I have to try to paraphrase Chaucer this is one of the impossible words, because in our so liberated age there is no way in English of expressing sorrowful emotion without, at the same time, efforts at self-defensive irony or humour.

One peculiar thing is that these necessarily ironical words do survive. You might expect that when people can no longer talk of 'ladies' and 'gentlemen' without sniggering the words would soon vanish from the language, but even a word as archaic as 'damsel' is in no actual danger of disappearing. Everyone understands the phrase 'a damsel in distress' though nobody can use it seriously. It is as if we preserve the word in order to destroy it.

The comparable funny thing is when people try to use straight words that really ought to be ironical. The speeches from the throne are a never failing source. In October 1974, Her Majesty was made to utter from the throne, in all the panoply of state, the words 'Proposals will be brought forward to tackle the abuses of the lump as a step towards creating a stable work-force in the construction industry'. She was also made to report her ministers' promise 'to provide more homes to rent'. I do wish the Queen had managed to speak those words ironically, because the lump is so much a slang phrase of the day that it ought not to be used solemnly, and phrases like 'homes to rent', 'home loans', 'selling new homes', will devalue the very important English notion of 'home', unless they are used as necessary ironies, sneers at the commercialism of those who make money by them. Because a 'home', unlike a house, can't be built, bought, rented or otherwise treated as an assemblage of physical objects. The final result of pretending it can will be that 'home' and 'homely' will go the way they already have in the United States and themselves become necessary ironies.

But the words I most want to see restricted to ironical use are from our utilitarian orthodoxy. It's high time it went the way of other orthodoxies. 'Pleasure', used of the dreary round of joyless indulgences provided by the 'entertainment industry'; 'compassionate' used of unfeeling people; 'growth' of the economy said with that breath of awe people used to reserve for the religious – they ought all to be sneered at, and the people who 'compassionately' demand export-led 'growth' to increase happiness ought to be met with the final comment of laughter.

I even hope to live to see the day when nobody will be able to use the word 'counter-productive' or the phrase 'male chauvinist pigsty', which I came on in *The Times*, without provoking giggles.

Felicitudes

In the Jerusalem Bible, the Roman Catholic mid-Atlantic version in use throughout the American-speaking world, Jesus begins the 'Evangelical Discourse' formerly known as the Sermon on the Mount with the following whopping untruth:

> 'How happy are the poor in spirit;
> theirs is the kingdom of Heaven.
> Happy the gentle:
> they shall have the earth for their heritage.'

'Poor in spirit' is hardly a current English phrase, except as a Bible quotation. Perhaps it could be used of someone dingily depressed by being jobless, or of someone who preferred being ordered about to being free, or of people who tamely submit to insults. 'That's a poor-spirited chap', some people might say. However we understand the phrase, to call someone 'poor in spirit'. 'Happy' in our English is just nonsense. By happiness we mean nowadays something more like satisfaction or abandonment to pleasurable activity. The *Guardian*, for instance, neatly married egalitarianism with our kind of 'happiness' when greeting the new year of 1974. It then proclaimed 'equality of satisfaction' as the great human aim. And we all know when we are happy. I agree with Bentham as against John Stuart Mill here: I don't believe it makes any sense to tell a man, 'you may think you feel you are miserable but really you are happy'. In our age, it is raging nonsense to say that anyone is happy if persecuted. The Jerusalem Bible does say so:

> 'Happy are those who are persecuted in the cause of right:
> theirs is the kingdom of heaven.'

Well, that takes my breath away. One may admire the heroism of those who have survived persecution and even turned it to good. I think of Solzhenitsyn.

> 'O goodness infinite, goodness immense!
> That all this good of evil shall produce,

And evil turn to good: more wonderful
Then that by which creation first brought forth
Light out of darkness . . . '

Yes indeed. But happy? To say that anyone could be happy in
the camps of Stalin's Russia or the cancer wards out of which
Solzhenitsyn made those wonderful novels – the shallowness
of that makes me gasp!

The language of religion has been taken over by the language of the greatest-happiness-principle and has been reduced to nonsense by it. The King James Bible of 1611, of
course didn't talk about happiness. The deep difference is
expressed in one word, blessed.

> 'Blessed are ye, when men shall revile you, and
> persecute you, and say all manner of evil against
> you falsely, for my sake.
> Rejoice, and be exceeding glad: for great is
> your reward in heaven: for so persecuted they the
> prophets which were before you.'

But nobody is 'happy' to be abused and calumniated; nobody
likes being tortured or even being called a fool and knave by
an official press (or, for that matter, by Western 'public
opinion'). If one did enjoy the persecution it would not be
itself: a martyr who *wants* to be martyred is a fake. Nevertheless, 'Blessed are ye, when men shall revile you, and per-
secute you'.

In the Bible 'blessed' logically comes before 'happy'.
When 'happy' is used it depends upon 'blessed'. The bea-
titudes have not been improved by being turned into felici-
tudes.

Eleanor Bron

A moderate corpse

You probably think of a corpse as a dead body. But for people in the theatre a corpse is the very grave misdemeanour of smiling or laughing out of character.

'Corpsing' originally was something you did to someone else; it meant to confuse or put out another actor in the course of a piece of business; 'to corpse' was slang in those days for to kill. Some actors find that corpsing can be infectious, and not only on stage. An audience is often delighted if they spot a moderate corpse and join in the joke – it is after all a spontaneous happening, what you go to the theatre for: something may go wrong. But this has led to the institution of the 'cod' or phoney corpse, a 'spontaneous' loss of control which occurs every evening on cue.

In contrast to the obscurity of 'corpsing', one word whose origins are only too horribly obvious is 'to dry'. Not only is it descriptive of the stemming of the flow of words, but also of the physiological sensation of the drying up of the rush of saliva to the mouth and blood to the brain, the sense that even if your mind ever started to function again there would be no spittle with which to formulate the words.

Another nightmare is to be 'off'. This doesn't only mean to be giving less than your best performance. It can mean to be sitting three flights above stage level in your dressing room doing a crossword puzzle and hearing your cue over the tannoy. Missing a cue when you're actually onstage is bad enough; being 'off' is unforgivable, and heart-stopping.

An altogether better place to be is, of course, 'upstage'. Upstage defines at first that level on stage farthest from the footlights and nearest the cyc, or back wall. Hence it becomes no fixed place but any spot on stage where one lucky actor is so placed that others on stage have to turn away from the audience to listen or talk to him. I've noticed it being used lately too as a camp description of someone who's stand-offish or aloof or grand. And of course from upstage comes the verb 'to upstage' someone, which a really gifted actor can do perfectly well from a downstage position with his back to the audience. This, by the way, is also a perfect situation from which to corpse everyone else. But an actor of this calibre probably will have no need to stoop to such tricks as corpsing nor to another one known as mugging. 'Mugging' is another last resort – it's pulling faces in order to get laughs. I have always assumed that it comes from 'ugly mug' and not from the current style of pedestrian highwaymen; but on second thoughts it does smack a little of the desperate action of hitting people over the head, metaphorically speaking, to get results. If you are good and lucky enough to get laughs you can milk them, if you know how, squeezing out as many as you can; and if you can do the same with curtain calls you probably deserve them.

Theatrical jargon is like any jargon, a semi-secret language designed to mystify the layman. In addition, it's not surprising that so much of the actor's private language, words like 'to corpse', 'to dry', 'to mug', has to do with things that go wrong on stage. Since acting is by its nature a creating of illusions, the actor more than anyone else needs special words to help him keep his audience from being disillusioned.

Strangers in our midst

It is always amazing to me how good we are, on the whole, at speaking our own language, even as children; what subtle distinctions we make, constantly, without effort or deliberation. Equally, it is astonishing how difficult it is for foreigners. Even after long years of study they rarely manage to speak flawlessly in a new tongue.

I taught English in a language school for a very short time, and one thing I found was that I had to keep producing rules to explain slight distinctions of meaning that I had always taken for granted. To take a tiny example: there's not all that much difference between 'I have to be there at eight', and 'I must be there at eight'; but there is a difference, and a native speaker can tell what it is, and when to make it. Though my students couldn't.

Sometimes, of course, it simply isn't possible to lay down any rule and you just have to shrug and insist that: 'we just wouldn't say that'. Besides, it's almost more fun when they do get it slightly wrong. I once received a tape from a charming Japanese who'd seen a film I was in. He introduced himself and displayed an extraordinarily wide knowledge of the English Theatre and what he called 'your English High Society' and he ended by begging me 'Please to send recording of your own peculiar voice'.

It's easy enough to smirk fondly at such little errors; I couldn't utter one syllable of Japanese. But mistakes like these allow us to go on feeling superior, in an affectionate sort of way – they remind us that we have effortlessly mastered something that is so difficult for outsiders. A grown person struggling with our language is charmingly disarmed. It is very difficult to assess foreign statesmen speaking English; they may seem inept or at a loss. On the other hand I wonder what the French made of Mr Heath's valiant refusal to make any concessions at all to the fact that he wasn't speaking English.

We British are very spoilt – so many people bother to learn

English and to use it. We hate the sensation of being so much at a loss, of being forced back into a second babyhood, with the tantrum-provoking frustrations that arise when we find ourselves thinking thoughts of a complexity far beyond our means of expressing them.

What is more we are very wary of anyone who can be taken for a native, whether he's an Englishman speaking a foreign language or a foreigner speaking ours. There's something not quite right about it, an ability to divide the mind and enter into another personality – which in a way you have to do to speak another language perfectly. It is suspect and threatening; it admits of the possibility of an undetected and undetectable stranger in our midst – a spy, a man from Mars. So we like our foreigners to be recognisably foreign and are reassured by their little slips and solecisms.

And yet the blurred utterances and slight distortions of strangers can have echoes and resonances that our poets and philosophers strive for in vain. A man I know, a merchant sailor, had been rescued from some local hazard by a Chinese, while he was on shore leave in Singapore. His new friend came briefly aboard for what might be their last meeting, as the ship waited on an uncertain tide. Then, leaving, clasped him by the hand and said:

'In case I no see you more – Hello!'

It makes the world go round

I was in a brilliant play once, by the American author Murray Shisgal, called *Luv*. The title, spelt 'l-u-v', of course sounds like love but isn't; and the piece was about the enormities of selfishness and ruthlessness and destruction which human beings carry out in the name of love. It demonstrated what love is not, and why the three little words 'I love you' can often sound more like a threat than a promise.

But though love as a concept is travestied and ridiculed and generally bandied about, as a word somehow it endures – vague and indestructible. Extraordinary claims are made for it – that it makes the world go round, for example and absence of it fills the law courts and the psychiatrists' offices.

And the word 'love' is applied to all sorts of things that at first sight may seem to have little or nothing in common. What is it about one's love of God, of work, country, parents or of a favourite food, that is shared by purely sexual love or indeed unhappy and unsexual romantic love?

The nearest I can come to pinning it down, is that it is a drive to find something to which we can give priority, usually something outside ourselves against which to measure ourselves – which in fact gives us the echo that confirms our existence. So love is something that gives shape and order to our lives. All the different forms of love confer a set of priorities and influence our behaviour, though some of them may be seen merely as an extension of self-love. Self-love, in moderation, is an ingredient for survival, but it can become a corruption of the urge towards order, turning us inwards so that we become our own priority.

This corrupt principle is responsible for a lot of the con-fusion and misunderstanding that surround the word 'love' True love, for instance, that so often goes awry. When two people really fall in love, as the saying goes, they willingly suppress any inconvenient facet of their natures, and simul-taneously turn a blind eye to any awkward aspects of their beloved. But this suppression becomes harder to maintain as time goes on – unless they are fortunate enough, as does happen – to have complementary egos. More often one ego ultimately refuses to continue giving priority to the other. Disappointed the lovers fall out of love. Love has failed to give meaning to their lives and that, in a way, is what all the various concepts which are covered by the single word 'love' are about: a drive towards meaning.

Of course a sense of over-riding purpose and of priority is produced by any form of strong passion. One reason why the seven deadly sins are so deadly is that they are seven passions which initially operate like love, providing meaning and purpose, but end by consuming and destroying, in disorder and chaos. Whereas love is distinguished from them by one essential characteristic: it creates order out of chaos. Which is what art does too, among other things. And which of course, for believers, is what God, in all his manifold forms, has always done.

When a modern civilisation laments the death of God, it's lamenting the disappearance of a secure and established order which seemed to exist before. God cannot help but be the ideal object of love, he is perfect by definition and by definition, therefore, must be more highly valued than ourselves. God *is* love, who made order out of chaos. If, in the beginning *was* the word, the word must have been 'love' . . . Perhaps it *is* love that makes the world go round.

John Weightman

Poetic acoustics

When Shakespeare wrote: 'A rose by any other name would smell as sweet', he was referring to what modern linguists call the arbitrary nature of the verbal sign or signifier. It is a historical accident that a rose should be called a rose in English, although we may think it a happy accident, since the roundness of the vowel and the modulation of the consonants from r to s may seem to correspond to the shape of the flower and to the impression of dewy freshness it produces at its peak. If, through some unhappy accident, the name of the rose had been 'artichoke', there would have been no difference in the scent of the flower, but English poets would have had a much more difficult time. There is not much that a modern English poet can do, for instance, in the way of the sublime, with that other beautiful and deliciously scented flower, the sweet pea. Walter De La Mare couldn't have used it to get the effect he achieves in:

> 'And no-one knows
> Through what wild centuries
> Roves back the rose.'

But the number of those words in English, as in any other language, which appear to be immediately appropriate to their meaning, is very limited; that is, the principle of onomatopaeia is of very little use in literature, because most words, as sounds, have no obvious connection with their sense. And yet we have an obscure feeling that good writing, especially good poetic writing, consists in establishing some correspondence between sense and sound. There is a philosophical paradox here: words are, for the most part, arbitrary, but good poetry makes them sound necessary. How does this come about? If I could answer the question fully, I would have solved one of the major mysteries of language. I have no hope of doing that, but I can perhaps make two relevant remarks based on my experience of the absolute untranslatability of poetry, at least as between English and French.

First, although poetry never resides entirely in any particular word, all poets tend to build up a vocabulary of favourite terms which fit into their acoustic systems. They have an emotional reaction to sound/sense combinations in the same way as different painters appreciate certain form/colour combinations. For instance, the poet, Paul Valéry, is especially fond of the French word for tree, *arbre*, possibly because the strength and vitality of organic growth is suggested by the two r sounds separated by a b. Now the English word 'tree', in comparison with *arbre*, is open-ended and rather wishy-washy, and can even set up an unfortunate echo of 'twee'. There is no hope, then, of translating Valéry's lines:

> 'Arbre, grand arbre, arbre des cieux,
> Irrésistible arbre des arbres.'

A literal rendering would be:

> 'Tree, great tree, tree of the heavens,
> Irresistible tree of trees.'

This may suggest the murmuring of the foliage, but not the strength of the organic structure. If we want to imply strength in relationship to a tree, we have to fall back on words like 'oak', 'trunk', 'root', and 'branch', which can be sturdily enunciated, but they cannot always be worked into the context.

Secondly, a good poet makes the sound/sense correspondence run through the line or phrase so that the meaning is supported and made resonant by the echo-pattern of the syllables. However, paradoxically enough, if the pattern is a shade too obvious, the poetry verges on the decorative, as often happens with Tennyson, possibly our greatest linguistic virtuoso after Shakespeare. But think of those lines in *In Memoriam*:

> 'And ghastly through the drizzling rain
> On the bald street breaks the blank day.'

They contain a stroke of genius, the flat monosyllabic echo of bald, break, blank, which is also a musical play on b-a-l, b-r-a and b-l-a, the sounds r and 1 being phonetic alternatives. Similarly, when Mallarmé, in his famous sonnet on Edgar Allen Poe, likens the poet's tomb to a meteorite: 'Calme bloc, ici-bas chu, de quelque désastre obscur', he achieves perfect expression by suggesting the mass of rock 'calme bloc,' its fall 'ici-bas chu,' and the cosmic rumble from which it emanated 'de quelque désastre obscur'. But both Tennyson and Mallarmé are quite untranslatable; the necessity of their utterance is inseparable from the language in which it is written.

Linguistic limbo

In working on translations, one often comes across what might be called 'ghost words', that is terms which still exist in the dictionary and are even used occasionally in writing or in conversation, but which have lost the full force of their original meaning, because of a change in social habits or in the material circumstances of life. They live on but most people have difficulty in giving them a definite meaning.

It was brought home to me the other day, for instance, that the word 'hoop' is no longer as significant as it used to be when I was young. In a novel by the French writer, Jules Romains, there is a very beautiful passage describing the lyrical experience of a little boy as he rolls or bowls his hoop through the streets of Paris, in the days of horse-drawn carriages. I have always been particularly fond of this description, because it expresses so exactly the feelings I had, a generation later, when I rolled a hoop through the streets of a provincial town in England. I set it not long ago as a translation-exercise for a class of eighteen-year-olds, and was surprised by their blank looks and uncertainty when we came to the expression *jouer au cerceau:* to play with or to bowl a hoop. It eventually turned out that, for them, to play with a hoop meant, in the first place, to have fun with a hoola hoop, something quite different from the activity described by the French author. A few said they remembered having seen pictures in old books of children bowling hoops, but not one had actually seen, or played with, a hoop of this kind. It then occurred to me, of course, that the development of the motor car has probably made it impossible for children to bowl hoops in the street as much as they used to do, and therefore the word is moribund in this sense, or even extinct in some areas; it has gone into the linguistic limbo, like hoop in hooped dress. Therefore, the passage I had selected as having an immediate appeal could only become intelligible to the class through an effort of imagination. Neither the experience nor the word was a living thing, and the text had got to the stage of needing an explanatory footnote.

There is nothing extraordinary about this; it is the usual process of linguistic wear and tear. But technological change is now taking place at such a rate that many more words and concepts may be affected than we think. Not long ago after the episode of the hoop, I had occasion to discuss the names and metaphorical significance of birds and, again to my surprise, I discovered that several young people had no knowledge of the habits of the lark; they couldn't say where it nested, in what circumstances it sang, or how big a bird it was. All they knew was the name. The lark was not part of their natural background, as it had been for Shelley when he wrote his ode, or Wordsworth when he composed his sonnet. I myself have never heard a nightingale in the flesh, but only in pre-war BBC broadcasts, and so Keats's ode has always been for me something of a literary exercise, without the direct effect of the two poems about the lark. It would be interesting to know how many young people have actually heard a cuckoo in nature, and can immediately see the point of the lines:

'O cuckoo, shall I call thee bird
Or but a wandering voice?'

Perhaps, with the development of battery farms, even the clucking of hens and the crowing of cocks will soon become abstract concepts, like the howling of wolves.

The mention of wolves is a reminder that some of these ghost terms remain surprisingly vigorous, even after the reality to which they correspond has disappeared. Wolves have vanished to all intents and purposes, and yet we still say: 'to keep the wolf from the door', 'to throw to the wolves', 'to cry wolf', and so on. We seem to need these metaphors, as we need 'a cuckoo in the nest' or 'up with the lark', but how long can they survive in a totally urbanised and industrialised society, which has to learn their meaning artificially? Already, I suspect, 'a cuckoo in the nest' no longer has its full sinister significance, which many people are probably unaware of, and has also been softened by the secondary implications of 'cuckoo', in the sense of dotty or crazy. Although we have almost entirely lost the pastoral background of life, we depend upon a ghost-like system of pastoral metaphors, which are now uncertain to some extent through being detached from their roots. The scientific revolution has not yet taken place in language.

The mystery of language

Words are one of the great mysteries that we have to live with from day to day. No-one knows how language came into being, that is, how man converted what must have been originally an animal cry into the complicated systems of articulate speech. We don't know what is happening when we speak; the words well up into consciousness from memory, but we don't understand how, and we have no control over the particular words which present themselves, apart from being able to disown them if we don't like them. As the old lady said: 'we cannot know what we think until we see what we say', and even then we may not believe what our own words are telling us, although the process of belief or disbelief is also a mystery. And, above all, we don't know why there should be so many languages or whether there is any common denominator between them. Does language really exist in the singular, like music, or are there only languages which must remain permanently foreign to each other, as long as they survive at all? Modern linguists are much concerned with this problem, but so far as I know, they are still a long way from solving it.

Given all these uncertainties, it is not surprising that a lot of people should yearn for linguistic simplification and should try to make words less endlessly complex than they are. This was the impulse behind the creation of artificial languages, such as Esperanto, which were meant to avoid the apparently unnecessary illogicalities of the natural languages. We haven't heard much about them in recent years, probably because, for the time being, Anglo-American is winning the race to become the world-language, since historical developments have made it the basic medium of politics and technology. But I am quite sure that if Esperanto had caught on, the sign of its success would have been that its words immediately began to develop complexities of meaning, as a ship in use grows barnacles.

In more recent times, when computers first became common, it was supposed that it would soon be possible to invent a translation-machine that would simplify the transference of word-meanings from one language to another. The pioneers quickly discovered that computer-translation is only feasible as between scientific vocabularies in which each term has a single meaning, and the relationship between the terms can be reduced to a simple, syntactical pattern. It would take a wise machine to recognise the relevant meaning of any ambiguous, everyday word in a natural language – try, for instance, imagining how it could be taught to distinguish between 'steps' and 'stairs' in English, or between the simple and continuous present 'I make', 'I am making'. The machine could not be cleverer than the linguists making it. Underlying the natural languages, it seemed clear that there must be a system of some kind, as yet unknown. At the same time, on the surface, almost everything often appears to be idiomatic, that is, unique and as it is, simply because that is the way things happen to be.

However, one of the comforting things one gradually learns through the practice of translation is that features of a given language which at first sight appear unnecessary and even exasperating, may on closer inspection prove to have advantages.

Take, for example, the survival in French of the division of the nouns into masculine and feminine and the rules of agreement with adjectives and past participles. This feature of the language is a great nuisance to English people learning French, but it never bothers a Frenchman, and the interesting point is that the division into genders makes it possible for French writers to achieve, quite instinctively, delicate effects of rhythm and balance through alternating masculine and feminine articles, pronouns and word-endings, effects that are often impossible to render in English. For instance, the apparently dull vowel 'e' – the so-called 'e mute', which occurs in so many feminine endings – is absolutely essential for the structure of French poetry. Genders may seem unnecessary, and illogical to the modern mind, but where they exist, the genius of the language can exploit them and thus give them, as it were, a secondary justification. This means that the criteria of usefulness in linguistic matters are not as easy to define as all that. The words of a given language are part of a great, baroque, proliferating structure, any part of which can suddenly be given a new, significant twist that no one had thought of before.

Christopher Driver

Taste the quality

For some time now we've been told that it's patriotic to buy British even if it makes us feel poorer. It must be time we started thinking of our language, too, as a marketable national asset. Try subjecting it to the kind of review it would get from time to time if it were a railway industry, or an oil deposit, or a computer software programme. What about research and development? Are we investing enough in English? Should we be trying to identify the particular things that we can't do very well with English, as opposed to all the marvellous things that we can?

Perhaps only a Frenchman normally thinks about his language like this, but we could always set up an English Language Development Committee – a little Noddy, it would have to be called. And it could well make a start with a subject in which the French have long had a lion's share of the market: cookery, and the critical vocabulary associated with the sense of taste. I know something about this, because as editor of the *Good Food Guide* I read several thousand reports every year from people trying to describe, praise, or damn the meals they have eaten in British hotels and restaurants. I've had to write my own reports too, and I sympathise with their difficulties.

There are two problems. In the first place the culinary art in Europe was refined and systematised by Frenchmen, who gave a precise meaning to terms and processes at a time when English practitioners, however able, were working chiefly by rule of thumb. So even apart from the tedium and risk of making a fool of yourself that arise when you swot up technical terms in a language you can't express yourself in, there's the evident fact that hardly any French dish sounds either as succinct or as succulent in English as it does in the language of its originator.

See how many words it takes an encyclopaedia to render in English, say, *timbale de sole Cardinal*: 'stuffed folded fillets of sole poached and served in a round china dish with sliced mushrooms and crayfish, coated with lobster sauce'. The same snag catches that other classically developed cuisine, the Chinese. In London Chinese restaurants you sometimes see on a menu descriptions such as 'boiled pig's hooves' or 'blubber' and it takes courage to penetrate behind this to something delicate, tasty, and traditional.

Then there's a second and in a way more obstinate problem. In English we have to do without the kind of vocabulary that might have evolved if as a nation over the past couple of centuries we'd been keen observers of culinary processes, and keen tasters of the results. For instance, while a casserole or a sauce is maturing it doesn't need to boil or even simmer: the French, noticing the slight creasing of the surface, say it 'smiles'. Twenty-five years ago the *Good Food Guide's* first editor, Raymond Postgate, used to complain that the British public could find little to say about dishes they had enjoyed except that the helpings were 'ample' and 'piping hot' (now 'piping hot' is a cliché that goes back to Chaucer, who must himself have stood close enough to an oven to notice the whistling noise from air trapped in a really incandescent dish).

In recent years cooking in many British households has become more sophisticated, and descriptions such as 'garlicky' or 'inadequately marinated' may appear in my postbag alongside plain evaluations such as 'delicious', 'calorific', or 'disgusting'. One recent correspondent – a left-wing politician, I was pleased to notice – even evoked for me 'a silky fish soup poised between clarity and gravity'. But more basic deficiencies remain. What do you say when you want to describe the texture that sprouts or spaghetti should have when cooked? 'Crunchy?' Too raw. 'Firm?' Only fit for a mousse. So it's back to *al dente*, and complaints from popular journalists that the *Guide* is preciously relying on foreign imports, the verbal equivalent of Chianti and Gorgonzola cheese.

A nice woofle underneath

From the point of view of a cook English is seriously underdeveloped. Vital descriptive words are missing, so we're forced into French or Italian to evoke the correct texture for an omelette or a dish of spaghetti – both long ago naturalised as items in our own diet. Are there other subject areas, though, of which the same is true? You'd expect them to be ones where taste and technique overlap, and where the British have trailed behind other nations for a century or two of linguistic evolution.

Serious music is an obvious example. That may sound odd today, when so many good composers and executants, some of them even of British origin, choose to live and work in these islands. But it was different in the last century, and even fifty years ago, a visiting German could publish a book about Britain called *The Land Without Music*, without being laughed at.

So the same trouble arises with the performance and appreciation of music as it does with the production and appreciation of meals; it's not all that easy to discuss it in English. It doesn't matter too much that the basic directions to performers are normally in Italian. Many of the terms are virtually English by now – what would political journalists do without 'crescendo' and 'fortissimo'? – and few British composers seem to have imitated Percy Grainger's vernacular instructions such as 'becoming louder' and 'pulling up a bit'. Besides, much contemporary music demands a wholly new notational language for publishers and conferences to wrangle over – or 'harmonise', as they would say in Brussels.

But what about the words that both critics and executants need at the tip of their tongues, to catch all the nuances of timbre, phrasing and style that make the difference between a routine and a distinguished performance of a piece of music? The other day, I went through a long gramophone record review by one of our most published music critics, listing the adjectives and phrases used to describe either the music itself or some aspect of its performance.

With very few exceptions, they were words that told me nothing at all about what the critic heard except that he liked it: 'evocative', 'magnificent', 'vital', 'beautiful', 'skilful', 'mellow', 'under-appreciated', 'striking', 'purposeful' ('striking' and 'purposeful' twice in the same paragraph), 'superb', 'loving', 'devoted', 'radiantly convincing' – and I will spare you the rest. Of course, a writer's very use of an adjective is often a confession of despair. In another critic's piece that caught my eye, nothing told me as much about the actual sound the London Symphony Orchestra made in an early Mozart symphony as his metaphorical description of 'this great Rolls Royce of an orchestra swinging down the country lanes and never once scratching its paint'. But once you've used a phrase like that, you can't repeat it the next night, and the night after, the way you can with 'glowing' or 'devoted'.

I doubt myself if the language of criticism can be enriched except by spreading round among its consumers a more subtle and detailed understanding of the techniques by which certain effects are obtained in the art concerned. Naturally, this takes many, many years, though for music, we ought soon to find an effect showing, now that so many young people are taught to play instruments decently, and now that so many of the world's best musicians – thanks mainly to Hitler – have English as their first language. Great conductors, it's true, generally manage to get their meaning across without any actual vocabulary at all, but it does help to possess the fluency and expressiveness of a Beecham at rehearsal. 'That tune of yours, flute, I want it played as if you heard someone whistling, walking away from you in the street, and suddenly turning a corner.'

The sheer stress of searching for a word to characterise a

sound, smell, or taste you have experienced or want to experience is itself a generator of linguistic diversity. Meaning is use, as Wittgenstein remarked, and here is what the writer John Moore overheard from a couple of Cotswold villagers discussing the relative ripeness of pears on different trees in an orchard: 'frum' meant ripe and in perfect condition; 'mawsey' meant soft and woolly. Similarly, it didn't take recording engineers long to invent 'wow' and 'flutter', and not long ago I heard an eminent string quartet leader saying at rehearsal: 'It's the viola's tune. It's not a question of the others playing more softly but of being woollier while she's ridgier. A nice woofle underneath her.' I wish critics wrote as helpfully as that.

Hymns and headlines

'O Bible chopped and crucified
in hymns we hear but do not read
none of the milder subtleties
of grace or art will sweeten those
stiff quatrains shovelled out four-square . . . '

Those lines from Robert Lowell's poem called *Waking Early Sunday Morning* stick to my mind for two reasons: first, I rather like hymns, and know it to be very difficult indeed to write a good one, especially in a generation as diffident about its religion as ours. Second, I've spent perhaps a thousand evenings in a newspaper composing room watching the man called a 'stonehand' literally chopping and shovelling metal lumps of words – paragraphs of type – to make them fit a column. When as a sub-editor you sent up for setting a headline too wide for the allotted measure you were guilty of unprofessional conduct, and you were told severely that it had 'bust'.

And hymn writers have something of the same problem. I doubt if a New England poet bearing the name of Lowell could write about the 'Bible chopped and crucified' without thinking of America's first printed book, the *Bay Psalm Book* of 1640. That was the Pilgrim Fathers' version of the metrical psalters, which the English Puritans had been using throughout the previous century, so that they could sing their favourite psalms to the tunes of Calvin. We sing some of them in my own church to this day, though in hymn books they have long been interspersed with more graceful verses by Watts, Wesley and others. For instance, this is what the metrical psalmist made of the phrase 'Like as the hart desireth the waterbrooks, so longeth my soul after thee, O God':

'Like as the hart doth pant and bray the well springs to
   obtain

So doth my soul desire alway with thee, Lord, to remain.'
I'm reminded that when you're writing words to fit a set space it's as embarrassing to have too much room to fill as too little. When the headline has to be short you easily fall into the canting language of Fleet Street – 'shock', 'probe', 'jobless' – or the kind of puns that set your teeth on edge. But with a longer line to write you may need to pad out by telling a bit of the story you're headlining, and not every tale lends itself to the fantasy of condensation the *Guardian* once achieved with the headline 'Man speaking little English lost with five unfed bears'. More often, if you try to tell a story in a headline, English syntax trips you up, as in the headline I collected from the same paper the other day: 'Man rebuked over baby listed for top job'.

By speaking affectionately of both hymns and headlines, I suppose I'm contending that for words to surrender their flavour, to *tell* properly, they need the constraint of a set length, form or measure. Newspapers, it's often said in the trade, were better written when newsprint was rationed, and, in another context, think how much pleasure the English take in that exacting little form the limerick, and the Japanese in *haiku*, which allow you only seventeen syllables to say something memorable in. Hymns, too, outlast and out-influence most theology partly, of course, because they come complete with tunes, but also because their writers have had to make up their minds to say one thing and say it clearly without any ifs and buts. Rhyme and metre both compel them to use short words like hope, joy, peace rather than portmanteau ones like justification and demythologisation. The best Robert Lowell could say for hymns, in that stanza I quoted at the beginning, was that:

> 'they gave darkness some control
> and left a loophole for the soul.'

But notice how a master of the craft, Isaac Watts, rises to what you might think an insuperable task, versifying the 23rd Psalm. He rounds it off in monosyllables and in a striking image that is true to experience, if not to the original:

> 'There would I find a settled rest
> While others go and come
> No more a stranger or a guest
> But like a child at home.'

If Watts had lived in the twentieth century, he'd never have got into the Church. The *Mirror* would have snapped him up.

Verbal violence

In the early twenties of the last century, a group of soldiers entered a pub in a Lancashire mill town. Some men on strike were already drinking there, and the soldiers had been despatched to the town to break their strike. This sudden military incursion into the public bar caused one of the strikers to raise his glass and, in a loud voice, propose the following toast: 'That every one of the lice-infested, flea-jumping hairs on the head of each and every fusilier present should be split, that every one of their dull and thick bones should be broken, that each fusilier should then be tied to a stake in the town square and their grimy and sweaty skins flayed off their backs, and, while they still lived, their pimply skins should be hung in the sun till they dried, and then wrapped around a great drum which all the town should joyously beat as they danced at the soldiers' mass funeral.' All the strikers drank to this modest proposal. A soldier then remarked that the last speaker was a 'pigeon-toed, splay-footed, swollen-ankled, knock-kneed, ricketty-hipped, slip-disced, pigeon-chested, slope-shouldered, corkscrew-necked, slack-jawed, hook-nosed, cross-eyed, low-browed, bird-brained . . .' Such excellent parliamentary debate continued awhile, each side cheering their latest verbal athlete and then drinking to his particular and peculiar toast and when, after about an hour, the real business of the afternoon arrived – namely, a punch-up – both sides were too exhausted and too drunk to do anything about it.

Few would even bother to deny that there has been a shocking and indeed lamentable decline in the standards of English swearing. Before the Reformation, Catholics had myriads of saints and devils and mystical hierarchies through which they could methodically hound the luckless person whose soul they were damning: 'May his soul rot a seed a day in hell'; 'Before he dies may he crawl on all fours across the floor like a spider'. The Elizabethans maintained these high standards, even elevating cursing, the poor man's poetry, to the status of high art – they renamed it 'flyting'. In an age famous for its sport – bear baiting, bull running, cock fighting, pig wrestling, and chicken hurling – swearing matches were held in public houses and streets between well-matched opponents. Each contestant was given a minute in which to cuss out his opponent, and then had to stand back amicably while his opponent replied. Crowds gathered, took up sides, and threw money in the hat, until one contestant either dropped through exhaustion or was so dumbfounded he could think of no suitable reply. English swearing was reduced to its present barren repetition of four-letter words amongst the working classes by the obscenities of the Industrial Revolution, and amongst the upper classes by the obscenities of the first world war.

Until very recently verbal violence often took the place of physical violence. Primitive people always appear so barbaric to us because they look so fearsome – they are literally dressed to kill – and because their epic poems and histories are filled with gruesome and bloodthirsty 'Old Testament' descriptions of battlefields and victories over neighbouring tribes. When anthropologists have attempted to discover precisely what took place, however, on these hallowed battlegrounds, a very different picture emerges. Hours would be spent before battle while witchdoctors ritually and exhaustively damned the other side, to the wild football-supporter cheers of their own. Eventually, the two highly emotional and vocal armies would wobble in the general direction of each other. At extreme weapon range, two or three brave souls from each side would then dart forward and hurl their spears, resulting in one or two generally minor injuries to the other side. Honour thus vindicated and heroism proved, both sides would get down to the real purpose of battle, namely, rushing back home and composing bloodcurdling epic poems extolling their bravery and heroism – an ancient version of war memoirs.

Today, this verbal violence has been replaced with a regime of immaculately pacific behaviour and personal politeness. But in order to maintain the civilised calm of this rule, it has been found necessary to hang over the head of every man, woman, and child, on this planet sixteen tons of TNT – just to remind him to stay peaceable.

Language should always be powerful enough to transform, to transcend, a situation, to allow emotions and prides to be resolved in a dignified and forceful manner. At a time when the maxim 'jaw-jaw' rather than 'war-war' was never more apposite – we're running out of words.

Ingenious malapropisms

I live in a chapel, and so have a graveyard for a front garden. One day I was gawping at it with a friend. 'I zuppose thee 'ad un deconcentrated,' he said. I were I bit bewildernessed. 'I c'n bemember,' he went on, 'the last body buried here – Joseph Bigg. Him were a braggocious soul. He were in this puberlick house, zee, 'alf puggled, 'ad a jangle wi' the landlord, got in a gert pother, muggled out disregardless, an' ended up in the accidental ward.'

Although the lamentable Norman Conquest took place some 900 years ago, to listen to most Englishmen until quite recently you would never have known it took place, since they continued proudly and happily to speak a slow, lazy, and glorious Anglo-Saxon – in several hundred different dialects and often spiced with the most ingenious malapropisms.

An illiterate person is especially likely to be a master practitioner of language, since speaking is his only means of communicating and garnering information. If you 'pass the time of day' with a country person, he will drain your memory as dry as Pimlico Marshes; as you stand there he will shamelessly ransack and rifle your brain for information and news of the outside world, for he is a professional communicator. In a free-for-all clack-magging gossip-cum-general-information-exchange-and-mart, with belly rubbing belly, one arm over your shoulder and the other digging you in the ribs, contact is made, communication can commence. Full frontal Anglo-Saxon is no mere polite barrier like modern standard English, it expresses, presses out, forces out practical, vital vivid meaning. People waddle, waggle, fiddle-faddle, straggle, saunter, muggle, mingle, muddle, puddle, paddle, potter, patter, bristle, 'n' bustle. Some stagger zigger zagger, sozzled, boggled, plastered, blotto, buggared, puzzled an' puggled. All the words resonate with their meanings.

Anglo-Saxon is built like a cart-horse, but, for all its massive strength and sureness of muscle, like a thoroughbred Clydesdale or Suffolk punch, it can dop, dance, slide along a furrow or a swarve as delicately and softly as a light scad o' rain. 'Don't trust so an' so, a sniggles behind y back.' Watch a great steaming vat of boiling, seething, scuthering water, see how the great eddies and bubbles wobble and walm and moil up to the surface.

Good language should be wedded, welded to life. Where would we be without people like the ones who were described to me recently as 'descending on a meal like a flock of vouchers!' Which gets me back to 'malsyprops'. The art of creatively muddling words used to be widespread through the south of England, as widespread as – outdoor lavitation. It came with a slower, more leisurely way of life, and it revealed a delight in juggling and jumbling words, using language as a highly idiosyncratic and imaginative way of direct face-to-face communication. Unlike modern punning and word-play, which usually self-consciously forces itself into a conversation and ruins it, the old-fashioned, illiterate Anglo-Saxon malsyprop walms, muggles, moils up to the surface as unselfconsciously as a trout taking a fly.

Hope thee bin consecratin'.

Words from the scaffold

One of the least democratic aspects of modern mass execution techniques is the denial to the condemned of his ancient privilege of addressing the crowd gathered around the tragical stage of his scaffold. Before the Monmouth rebels' translation, before their literal discorporation by hanging, drawing, and quartering, each of the condemned West Country rebels seized the opportunity, upon 'the very brink of a great and stupendious eternitie', of hammering out, of expressing, of expounding their convictions and beliefs to their audience. Colonel Holmes, the Fifth Monarchist, incouraged and inspired his suffering brethren to hold out to the end, and not to waver, observing that 'this being a Glorious Sun-Shining Day, I doubt not, though our breakfast be sharp and bitter, it will prepare us, and make us meet for a comfortable supper . . .'

In many traditional cultures people have believed that they can actually become like gods, with all the powers a deity possesses, if only they can penetrate the ancient mysteries of language. Colonel Holmes, perched on his scaffold, was in as good a position as anyone ever has been, to evaluate the relationship between the physical and the spiritual.

It is my firm conviction, that in the bones, the belly and bowels of the English language there still reside certain wondrous, occult properties, an almost mystical co-mingling of the physical and the spiritual, and that a halfway competent word-wright, by a correct casting of his words, can dissolve in his audience the accepted boundaries between physical and spiritual, can transform, inspire them. Colonel Holmes, on his scaffold, inspired his fellow sufferers, he literally breathed fire into them – inspire – he couraged them by pouring courage into their shaking frames – incourage. On his tragical stage, he expressed, pressed out, expounded, pounded out his own spirit. 'Upon the brink of a great and stupendious eternitie', as the butchered quarters and bowels and hearts and privates and heads of his previously expired companions smoked around him, Colonel Holmes galvanised, actualised, realised, transformed, transfigured, even, dare I say it, put new heart into those who were to follow him.

The Fifth Monarchists and innumerable other Civil War sects subscribed to that most ancient of English heresies, the Pelagian heresy, the belief that instead of original sin man is born in original virtue, that paradise is here and now, and that one witnesses in everyday life, 'the human face divine'. John Milton's angels – spiritual beings without sin who can still experience all the joys of the flesh – 'comingle' their bodies in lovemaking, like summer clouds, can totally enter each other and become as one. 'In the hot bowels of love,' as the Fifth Monarchists had it, physical and spiritual are welded and wedded together, and the English language not only reflects, but actively conspires towards this union.

On Lyme Regis shore, the one-armed Colonel Holmes – his right arm had been shattered in battle and he'd cut it off himself with an axe on a kitchen table – had to be helped up the ladder by the executioner. The executioner offered to take off his chains, but the Colonel considered that 'Great men of state wear chains, and 'tis accounted for their honour, and though there is a vast difference between those golden ones and mine, yet I take mine to be more honourable'. And so, perched precariously on the top of the ladder, the one-armed and thus 'imperfect' Colonel Holmes made his final joke – 'I doubt not, that though our breakfast be sharp and bitter, it will prepare us, and make us meet for a comfortable supper.' Not only does he look forward to being reunited with his comrades in heaven, but, with a typically grisly Fifth Monarchist delight in word play, he sees his body as the meat, the flesh, upon the divine communion altar. Thus, using the explosive potential of the English language as propellant, Colonel Holmes launched himself into that 'great and stupendious eternitie'.

Dannie Abse

Innocent misunderstandings

'I'll expect you next Wednesday,' I had said. She never arrived. When I phoned her later, she said, 'Oh dear, a verbal misunderstanding. You should have said this Wednesday. By next Wednesday I assumed you meant the Wednesday of the following week.' After I put down the phone I recalled that rather poor joke about the three half-deaf passengers travelling through the West Midlands. As the train slowed the first passenger asked, 'Is this Wednesbury?' 'No, Thursday,' the second passenger, Bill, replied. And the third passenger, Mel, continued, 'I could do with a drink too.'

But why did my friend misinterpret 'next Wednesday'? Unconsciously did she wish to postpone our date? After all, a slip of the tongue, Freud teaches us, may reveal a telling and unsuspected significance. And so, perhaps, verbal misunderstandings, too, may suggest purposes, desires, the listener may not consciously acknowledge. Consider Mel, the third half-deaf man who had said, 'I could do with a drink too.' Doubtless, he was a lover of alcohol, if not an alcoholic! He did not want to hear Bill tell him the day of the week. Rather he wanted to hear the heart-rending cry of a fellow tippler.

Of course, not all verbal misunderstandings result from unconscious longings or negations. One can settle a pillow or turn towards the window and echoing T. S. Eliot say, 'That is not it at all, that is not what I meant at all,' without narrowing one's eyes in a paranoid way. Eliot himself had cause to complain of innocent verbal misunderstandings of his work. One of Eliot's poems, *Journey of the Magi*, begins:

    'A cold coming we had of it
    Just the worst time of the year
    For a journey, and such a long journey . . . '

These lines were translated into German so that they signified:

    'We had a cold coming
    Just at the worst time of the year
    For a journey, and such a long journey . . . '

It is unlikely that the translator wished to diminish Eliot, or that as he translated these lines he happened to suffer from a particularly heavy and depressing head cold. No, he was just ignorant.

And sometimes we have reason to be grateful for such ignorance. Unforgettable passages in the King James Bible prove my point. Marvellous constructions also arise from verbal misconceptions. Even the unicorn is probably a mistranslation from the Hebrew, and without that fabulous beast so many paintings would be blank, so many tapestries never begun, so many poems deleted. George Barker's assertion that unicorns don't exist because they have better things to do is an amusing lovely slander. They *do* exist, and we are richer for them and all because of a verbal misapprehension.

Yet some purists believe it's better not to understand a language at all than to understand it imperfectly. To be sure, I can think of one occasion when I could have argued this brief. I had attended a writers' conference in Israel and afterwards was invited along with an Israeli writer to discuss the proceedings on radio. First I was to speak in English; then the Israeli writer would respond in Hebrew. 'Then, Mr Abse,' said the radio producer, 'you take up the thread and so on and so forth. I would like a first class argument.' I pointed out that, alas, I wouldn't be able to understand one word the Israeli writer said for I had no Hebrew. The producer hesitated only for a moment. 'You're a poet,' he said, 'use your imagination'.

So I spoke for a minute, listened to a language I couldn't

understand for a minute, then rebutted what I hoped the Israeli writer had said. We continued our argument for a quarter of an hour, and after the broadcast the producer embraced us both. 'Beautiful,' he shouted, 'beautiful.' No doubt our Hebrew-English dialogue was a symbolic political parable of some kind. Anyway, deaf man spoke to deaf man that Wednesday and we all went off for a drink.

Ceremonial insincerities

There are words used in certain contexts that have become inert, even dead. We sit down to write a letter, and address a friend, a stranger, or even an individual we actively dislike, with a 'Dear'. 'Dear Fred', we write, or 'Dear Mr Smith', or 'Dear Fred Smith', or 'Dear Smith', when Smith is not dear to us at all, never had been, never will be. We write 'Dear' with as little sincerity as those authors of the Tel Armana letters who, more than three thousand years ago, commenced their letters with a 'Seven times by seven times I fall at your feet'. But those once inert words, because they are no longer used, have become alive again. A meaningless formal ceremonial beginning to a letter has become a line of a poem.

If we are ignorant of the ceremonial language-gestures of a particular society we are likely to react to them freshly. I recall the first time I visited the United States. When served my first breakfast by an attractive American waitress I felt I was in a movie. When she passed me the orange juice I automatically thanked her. 'You're welcome,' she replied. How sweet of her, I thought, to react like that and at this time of the morning. I wished to thank her for saying I was welcome, to show my gratitude for her generosity of spirit. So I said again with warmth, 'Thank you,' and again she responded, not looking at me now, 'You're welcome.' This time I repeated my 'Thank you,' less ardently. 'You're welcome,' she said like a taped answering service. I was just beginning to experience a mild depression when, suddenly, all was dazzle and sunlight once more. For, with remarkable open warmth, the waitress even as she handed me the bill said, 'Now you have a nice day.'

The Americans use a vivid phrase: 'She came on a bit strong'. But all Americans, as far as we British are concerned, come on a bit strong. It doesn't matter a jot, of course, providing we understand the nuances of their statements: that what they say they don't necessarily mean any more than we do. I used to be pleased when an American friend wrote, 'Thank you for your good letter'. Later, though, several other American correspondents thanked me for my good letters and gradually I realised that they no more meant it than I did when I asked them to convey my greetings to their *good* ladies whom I secretly suspected may well have been bitches or harlots.

Yet the ancients 'came on' more strong than any contemporary American. Here is the opening of a letter dictated by Abimelech of Tyre to Amenhotep IV about 1370 BC:

'To the King, my lord, my pantheon, my sun-god say: Thus Abimelech, thy servant. Seven and seven times I fall at the feet of the King, my lord. I am the dirt under the feet of the King, my lord. My lord is the sun-god who rises over the lands day by day, as ordained by his gracious father: who sets the whole land at peace by his might, who utters his battle-cry in heaven like Baal so that the whole land quakes at his cry . . . '

This is but the beginning of the letter, or, as we say nowadays, 'That's just for starters'. All Abimelech has to tell Amenhotep is: 'I am guarding Tyre until you, the King, arrive.' The rest is wrapping. It makes the American, 'You're welcome,' and 'Have a good day,' perfunctory, even rude.

Our own verbal insincerities are so commonplace we do not notice them and those we address know we know that they know we do not mean what we say. 'Do call in on us when next you visit Reading,' said Fred Smith to my wife and me. And supposing one evening, about dinner time, we did happen to be in Reading with our three children, and did knock on his door to announce, 'We're here. Hello Fred!' I can imagine the candid traumatic look on his face. Ah, but he would find the right, inert, dead words soon enough, the correct ceremonial response that would allow him legitimately to pretend to feelings he did not own or to conceal feelings he would rather not openly display. Yes, he would say blandly, 'How very nice to see you,' and call his stunned wife from the kitchen where several pots on the stove were about to over-brim. And she too, shaking hands with my family, and despite her headache and sore throat, would respond to our 'How are you?' with a smile and a 'Fine, *fine*, thank you!'

Verbal swank

'Even if you don't recall in detail Robert Southey's *Life of Nelson 1813*, you would have read, surely, Southey's poem *Madoc*. You know, about Madog ab Owain Gwynedd?' Well, rather than admit a defeated, self-shaming 'No', many of us prevaricate when confronted with such a challenging and pulverising monologue. We grunt an ambiguous, 'Mmm,' or maybe flex the head gently in a non-committal modest way, or brazenly come out with a 'yes' in a stretched voice. All display of obscure erudition leaves us a little resentful. Our own ignorance is too rawly exposed; the superiority of our friend and adversary in conversation too openly affirmed.

We feel similarly towards those who have 'swallowed a dictionary,' whose vocabulary is wide and idiosyncratic and whose expression of it fluent. An ostentation of vocabulary, spoken or written, arouses in us feelings of envy and of admiration. Look at my word-hoard, some writers (men more often than women) seem to insist, as if they were pointing to their new white Rolls Royce or at their wife's diamond as big as the Ritz or, more directly, to their own exposed outsize genitals. And some of us, perhaps, are suitably crushed. But isn't that the intention, or at least the unconscious motive, of the lexical author? A man who deliberately uses words that others are likely to be ignorant of is committing a minor act of aggression, and in so doing would inform us of his power and superiority.

There are some writers I admire even though they constantly use uncommon words. In reading the late poems of Auden I have often had to extend my arm laterally for a dictionary to look up words such as 'nisus' and 'ensorcelling'. If writers do display a rich vocabulary, however irritated we may be at their verbal swank, this very richness does argue for them an authority which we are persuaded to acknowledge. Authors like Aldous Huxley and Arthur Koestler who have occasionally peppered their prose with scientific-jargon words – 'neoplasm' instead of 'cancer', or even 'dermis' instead of 'skin' – perhaps have done so in order to achieve, though spuriously, a tone of authority.

Verbal ostentation is not confined to writers. The ego-clamour of any dinner-party conversation is likely to be quelled by an insistent doctor's voice saying, 'I saw a patient today suffering from sub-acute bacterial endocarditis.' A doctor, whatever his deficiencies in common knowledge, though he may never have heard of Auden, Huxley or Koestler, can by casually talking about, say, 'coccidiodomycosis' or 'sub-acute combined degeneration of the cord', reduce others with far more eclectic scholarship to a position of transient inferiority. The doctor-patient relationship is based on such a balance. If doctor and patient acknowledge each other as equals the patient would not recover so quickly and the doctor would become ill!

Because of this assumption, or rather presumption of superiority, the doctor in addressing a patient will simplify his word-hoard in a most transparent way. Observe how he strides into casualty and all the patients on the benches become silent except for the blind man who is saying, 'I 'ope if 'e gives me stitches, 'e'll numb it first, nurse.' Now our white-coated hero descends a step to address the first patient who happens to be a Nobel Prize winner with a breezy, 'Not to worry,' and 'Just a little prick,' and 'How's the waterworks?' He will not even ask for 'urine'. So he says to the patient, who because he is a patient has become temporarily illiterate, 'I'd like a sample.'

Of course, doctors being human like to lord it not only over patients but over fellow doctors. That is why you may, in the corridors of the hospital, happen on two consultants involved in warring discourse. The first consultant is saying: 'Have you by chance read I. Taylor and H. L. Duthie on bran tablets and diverticular disease?' And the second consultant, with fugitive eyes, is flexing his head gently in a most non-committal modest way.

Frederic Raphael

Amo, amas, amat

'As every schoolboy knows . . . ' What a common phrase that used to be! What does every schoolboy know today? Certainly not *amo, amas, amat* – the rudiments of a classical education can no longer be assumed among the young, or even the young middle-aged. *Tempus fugit*. We all know what that means anyway. Yet when I was first at school, and it was not all that long ago, knowledge of the classical languages, Greek and Latin, was taken to be, as they now say, *ad nauseam*, what education was all about. *Amo, amas, amat* – I love, thou lovest, he or she loves – that simple conjugation was something every schoolboy did indeed know. I don't think it ever occurred to us to ask what every schoolgirl knew.

Curious really, that we began with the Latin verb for 'to love'. Love may have been a frequent subject in the poetry of Rome, but it was certainly not one on which, even long after puberty, we were expected to ask any practical questions, let alone to have any practical answers. We were never intended to treat the great texts as literature, as having a meaning which went beyond the unravelling of abstruse phrases and arcane references.

Of all the embarrassing texts, Catullus was perhaps the most awkward for old-fashioned schoolmasters. The trouble was, of course, that he was sexy and he was often downright obscene, even by the most amiable definition. Censorship was the only answer. Some of his poems, every schoolboy would be wise to accept, were not the thing at all. And when we stumbled on one of his naughty lapses, we should look the other way and not encourage him to think that he had been clever. That sort of thing wasn't clever at all. The consequence, of course, was that we could not rest, some of us, until we had, with the aid of a low crib and lower imaginations, deciphered in full, or as full as we could manage, what it was that made him so disreputable. Yet an English school was not, in my experience at least, despite its salting of homosexual passions and its boasts of kissed popsies, quite the place in which to get the full feel of life in ancient Rome. Life, in the sexual sense, was not at all part of what most schoolboys knew. *Amo, amas, amat*, yes; I love, thou lovest, he or she loves: not yet, not unless you were very lucky indeed, and most of us were not.

Now, the more one reads Catullus, the clearer it becomes that his so-called lapses were an essential element of his world. Yet even the Oxford edition of 1961 omits the very same poems which embarrassed my Carthusian masters. The funny thing is that this prudish edition coincides pretty well with the end of the habit of classical education in this country. And by a further coincidence it comes at the beginning of a decade which brought more sexual freedom than this country had known since the Regency gave licence a bad name. Just at the time when the classics were abandoned as the common denominator of education, the English freed themselves of some of the shame and the taboos which for so long made nonsense of classical criticism. Though the schoolboy no longer cries *Pax* (does he?) when he has had enough of a fight, he has an easier attitude, a greater familiarity with the world of sex, and even of love perhaps, than we ever did. The world of bawdy rarely puzzles or appals him. Society, for better or worse (I think for better) speaks a much bolder language and it is one which, by ironic chance, should render much more accessible the coarsenesses, and even the subtleties, of the classical world. In translation we can now use, with a certain relish, the whole vocabulary of sexual response. The God, Eros, dominates the western consciousness in a manner only a fool or a prude can now deny or dispute.

Certainly we have a much more flashy and less inhibited vocabulary. Hence we can comprehend paganism not only more fully but with less self-consciousness. The irony is that our educational system has abandoned the classics just when they could be appreciated with more humour and freedom than ever before. Few schoolboys – or should I say schoolpersons? – now learn *amo, amas, amat,* but love in a variety of graphic terminologies is no longer an unspeakable subject. Schoolboys have, you might say, rediscovered the roots of life at the very moment when – so far as classical culture is concerned – they are being cut out from under them. But which of them knows that?

Neck verse

It is curious how certain phrases hang in the air, as it were, like the smile of the Cheshire cat, without either disappearing from the language or remaining in common speech. 'Benefit of clergy' is one such. I confess that I thought for a long time that it was something which certain occupants of double beds enjoyed and others did not, that it was, as it were, a certificate brandished at prudish hotelkeepers to establish that one could not properly be denied conjugal apartments. But, of course, when the phrase was really current, it had nothing whatever to do with due process of matrimony.

At my preparatory school, we had a series of volumes of English history in strip cartoon form. The section which gripped my scandalised imagination was devoted to the variety of methods of justice in the Middle Ages. I can still see the line drawing of a man about to grip a red hot iron bar. What were his burns to prove exactly? I think that it was believed that if his wounds healed within a certain period, then his word was proved good. Such, more or less, was 'trial by ordeal'. 'Trial by combat' had a much more summary illustration: one man flat on his back, the other erect and hence – no twist to this story – the winner. Justice was not the will of the stronger, as Plato's *Thrasymachus* argued, but the strength of the stronger. Of course the King's justice was eventually established; superstition and brute force yielded to more subtle forms of contest. One need not doubt that certain unfavoured classes of persons continued, as it were, to be done, but they were no longer quite so clearly seen to be done. Yet one extraordinary form of trial by ordeal, or at least appeal by ordeal, continued to be practised. Did you know – for I did not, until a recent reading of his life – that the great Ben Jonson was, as late as 1598, saved from the gallows, at the age of 26, by only one circumstance? He knew how to read.

He claimed, for that reason, 'Benefit of clergy'. Those who could make good such a claim were immune from the jurisdiction of the ordinary courts. Had Jonson not been able to do so, he would certainly have been hanged. He had killed an actor in a duel. He saved himself by the reading of what was called, with ghoulish precision, 'neck verse'. You did not, as one might suppose, have to be an ordained cleric in order to claim clerical privilege. Simply because he could read, Jonson suffered only the minor punishment of confiscation of his goods, which did not amount to much, and branding of the thumb. Were that now the penalty for running through a contumacious actor, or critic, I suspect not a few playwrights would have scorched thumbs today.

The clerical or religious courts are, of course, long gone, but is British justice entirely without vestiges of religiosity? The taking of the oath still lends a witness more credibility, in the eyes at least of certain judges, than does merely 'affirming'. And are not the judges themselves dressed in the style of secular priests? Their consultation of impressively bound books harks back, it is not hard to guess, to a time when the mere possession of books, and of the capacity to read them, was of itself proof of distinction and authority. The essential book was, of course, the Bible; it was on the ability to read the Gospel that 'Benefit of clergy' was originally based. Those who can read and interpret God's word are powerful witch-doctors indeed. As Mark Antony was prompt to appreciate, sole access to a will, whether God's or

Caesar's, confers unarguable powers. The capacity to read, however, is not always a certificate of reprieve: Russian prisoners captured by the Nazis in the 1941 and 1942 campaigns were executed when it was found they *could* read. Their literacy being proof that they belonged either to the Communist Party or to the government apparatus.

A High Court judge once asked me, at a party, what I thought was wrong with British justice. I answered, with alcoholic cheek, 'The tyranny of the well-spoken'. To my surprise, he agreed instantly. One may well ask what other form of tyranny would be preferable, but the charge still stands. The man who speaks the King's English in the King's – or the Queen's – court enjoys a certain residual 'Benefit of clergy'; he announces his class, his distinction. It won't gain him any blatant advantage, but the Cheshire cat may still smile faintly at him from the bench, the palest reminder of the days when a clerk in Holy Orders, or a glib playwright, could indeed thank God that he was not as other men – and read 'neck verse' to prove it!

Rhyme and reason

'He did it without rhyme or reason.' Rather like going out, one might infer, without belt or braces. The alternatives sound mutually exclusive: one needs one or the other, but hardly both. 'He acted without let or hindrance' has a similar ring to it, but here 'let' and 'hindrance' are not genuine alternatives at all, from contrasting ends of the verbal spectrum: they are synonyms, like rod, pole or perch. 'Let', however, does have the sound of a kind of permission, which suggests to me that when people speak of 'let or hindrance' they may sometimes imagine that they mean 'with or without permission', which is not at all the case. 'Let' is used here as squash players use it, when they claim a 'let', meaning that they have been impeded.

'Rhyme or reason' is certainly, one would say, a genuine pair of alternatives. No more tautologous than chalk and cheese. Only in the distant past was rhyme at the service of reason, or reason a habit with rhymers. Would Alexander Pope be an instance? If so, it proves that rage and reason are not incompatible. But certainly by the time of Erasmus Darwin, that indefatigable celebrant of the scientifico-industrial revolution, the use of rhyme to further reason had degenerated into a sort of skipping plod. The two cultures split rather decisively at that point. Darwin gave didacticism a bad name and we would regard it as highly comic had Crick and Watson, say, the discoverers of the Double Helix, elected to present their vital conclusions in the form of a verse epistle to the magazine *Nature*.

Yet rhyme and reason were not strangers in ancient societies. Didactic verse was a commonplace. If Hesiod's *Works And Days* did not rhyme exactly, his countryman's calendar was expressed in formal and hence easily memorable metre, and so too, of course, was the militant rationalism of the philosopher Epicurus. And that of Epicurus' greatest disciple, Lucretius, who thundered his master's message in magnificent hexameters which demanded that his readers, or hearers, be guided by the most prosaic common sense and that they dismiss all superstition, however poetic, from their minds. Lucretius, for all his great emotional force, was a reasoner before he was a rhymer. He wrote to convince men that they were perishable, mundane creatures, without a future life or divine attention, though he may himself have had some small sense of his own imperishable qualities. Even so fierce a political conscience as Shelley's found Lucretius' didacticism unpoetical and his reputation has suffered for all of his propagandistic enthusiasm. We have come to believe that it is unaesthetic when art is made the vehicle of overt opinion. It suits us to make a divisive distinction between rhyme or poetics and reason and to insist that neither poaches on the territory of the other. Together they might prove too formidable an alliance. Plato was uneasy at the prospect of a poetic presence in his Ideal Republic. Poetry was too sly in rendering palatable disreputable stories which the Guardians were not disposed to swallow. Yet Plato himself, in a metaphorical sense at least, used both rhyme and reason. Could one not well argue, after all, that his *Myths* were prose poems? His apprehension of the power of the poet was the consequence, we need scarcely doubt, of how much he himself had smuggled through the gate of reason under the wide cloak of the muse.

'Rhyme or reason' is, anyway, not really a reliable antithesis. It is hard to resist the feeling that rhyme *is* a kind of reason. Rhyme in the basic noon-moon-June sense. Alexander Pope gave his couplets an incontrovertible quality by the use of rhyme. (Hence, I think, its prevalence in satire.) Could any blank verse aphorism be quite so clinching as:

> 'A little knowledge is a dangerous thing,
> Drink deep or taste not of the Pierian spring'

Nothing sharpens an old saw like a toothsome rhyme. The use of rhyme as a means of puncturing disparagement is really unrivalled. One thinks of Belloc's attack on the 'remote and ineffectual Don who dared attack my Chesterton' and of Chesterton's own 'Chuck it, Smith,' a supreme example of English contempt. Such rhymes give a poetic argument the unquestionable conclusiveness of a syllogism. The rhyming verse which most appeals to the modern ear is, I suppose, that with an ironic or sardonic purpose. Byron's *Don Juan*, for all its apparent self-centredness, remains an unsurpassed attack on social and political cant. No wonder authoritarians dread the conjunction of the rhymer and the rationalist. When a man acts with rhyme *and* reason, he is a potent opponent indeed. His voice is liable to be heard despite let or hindrance.

John Ziman

Naming physics

Scientists fall in love with their own creations – the words they have to make up for what they find in nature. In 1834, Michael Faraday needed words to describe what happens when an electric current flows through a chemical solution. Not having had a classical education, he consulted Dr William Whewell of Trinity College, Cambridge, the acknowledged expert on naming things in pseudo-Greek. The geologists had come away from Whewell well supplied with words like 'pliocene', 'miocene' and 'eocene': he would be happy to oblige the distinguished physicist. In a delightful exchange of letters Faraday describes the phenomena and explains concepts which he wished to express in the archaic abstractions of artificial Greek. Whewell offered several alternatives, including some barbarous tongue-twisters, such as 'skaiostechion' and 'cetazetode', that would have killed the science of electro-chemistry on the spot. Fortunately, Faraday was a man of natural good taste and agreed with Whewell's first preference for those beautiful words 'anode' and 'cathode', which are perfectly good Greek for 'the way up' and 'the way down', through which the mysterious particles, the 'ions', would pass. Now, after a century of physics and electronics, plus several extensions, generalisations and metaphors, we have in almost every home a cathode ray tube, on which magical pictures come and go.

Modern science has no time for such high-mindedness and linguistic delicacy; the names we get now for new scientific concepts commend themselves chiefly by their whimsicality or vulgarity. Yet the christening is occasionally graced with vitality and wit. Back in the 1950s, the big machines of high energy physics were producing whole families of elementary particles – dozens of them, interacting and decaying into one another with astonishing facility. Amongst them, however, there were some strangers that didn't combine readily with ordinary, everyday, protons and neutrons, but seemed to keep themselves to themselves. What enigmatic quantity distinguishes these particles? What can they call such an attribute, with, it seems, no other handle by which we might grasp it physically? Forget your Greek and go to the international vernacular of modern science. From now on the English word 'strangeness' shall be the name of what is to be added together and equated in such reactions. So now it is not just comical pedantry to say of a neutron or a proton that it has 'strangeness quantum number zero' to show how very ordinary and commonplace it is! It is a scientific statement, pregnant with inner meaning.

Recently the same problem arose in connection with the various families of quarks. Why are some particles much more stable than others? The latest experiments confirm the hypothesis that some quarks have a special property called 'charm', which must never be forgotten or changed. Indeed, the latest exciting discovery in high energy physics may be 'charmonium' itself, an ideal partnership of a 'charmed' quark and an 'anti-charmed' quark, waltzing around one another in sublime perfection until, after what seems an inordinately long life – a 'charmed' life, we might say – their mutual suicide pact carries them away in a flash of radiation. Oh shade of William Whewell; forgive us our barbarism in our scientific Tower of Babel!

'Quark' sounds like the cry of a seagull. So perhaps James Joyce meant when he began a new chapter of *Finnigan's Wake*, 'Three quarks for Muster Mark'. Mark was evidently King Mark of *Tristan and Isolde*, on a voyage. But Joyce could not have been unaware that 'quark' is the German word for soft cheese or, metaphorically, for rubbish. Murray

Gell-Mann chose this word in 1964 for the hypothetical entities that go in threes to make a proton, giving no more than the page reference to *Finnigan's Wake*. The defining phrase is quoted widely, but I must admit that until I checked all the commentaries standing side-by-side in academic order on the shelf in the university library, I thought it must be a 'kwork', a measure of drink, something ancient and Irish, three of them to the gallon, a superior 'quart' for a superior boozer in a splendid Dublin tavern. It's good to know that those who hunted the 'quark', with linear accelerators and bubble chambers need no longer fear that it is a cousin of the enigmatic 'snark', which was, of course, a Boojum, and never was seen again.

Of all the naming myths, I prefer the spontaneous response of Enrico Fermi, the great Italian physicist. In the 1930s there was talk of a new neutral particle to explain radioactive decay: could it be the 'neutron', recently discovered by Chadwick. 'No, no,' said Fermi. 'This is not Chadwick's neutron. It is a small neutron. It is a very, very small neutron. It is – it is – a neut*rino*.' And so it has been, to physics, ever since: bastard of Greek and an Italian diminutive, but alive and well, thank you very much, in our enigmatic universe.

In the beginning

To the petty professorial pedant composing his scintillating monthly letter to *The Times*, the proliferation of strings of initials like NATO, NALGO and UNCTAD is a barbarism to be profoundly deplored. But since this usage had evidently come to stay, why not lie back and enjoy it.

Anyway, what's good, or honest, in a title such as 'The National Economic Development Council'? Much healthier to call it the NEDC; or, better still, call it 'Neddie', and it's a friendly, bumbling stable companion for David Low's cart-horse of a TUC – sorry – the Trades Union Congress. We shall know that 'Neddie' has really succeeded when we have become so accustomed to it that we forget the origin of its name, and incorporate it, like the Board of Trade or the Privy Council, into our unwritten constitution. And who recalls, nowadays, that 'Ernie', the happy hobgoblin of good fortune who casts lots of prizes for our Premium Bonds, began his mischievous life as an Electronic Random Number something or other – just a mindless, soulless machine.

But there are times when we need new names for quite unprecedented concepts, or devices, or institutions. Gestapo and Gulag are horror acronyms, from abstract initials: Ian Fleming did his best with SMERSH; but no fictional organisation can sound like the NKVD for perfect nastiness. On the other hand, the CIA doesn't strike a chill or terror; the initials are too soft, too much like those of some Italian or Spanish corporation manufacturing mineral water or soap. UNESCO, however, is brilliant; surely this is a word from Esperanto, not to be found in any single language, but invented to describe any wallowing herbivorous mammal, useless for domestic drudgery, uttering occasional plaintive wails of protest, and overflowing with unnutritious milk from a plethora of tiny udders.

Admittedly, this proliferation of initials can become a disease. The Victorians managed very well with a few stable, conventional abbreviations, such as MP and KCMG. But their institutional world was simpler; bureaucracy had not taken over the civil services, the army, or the industrial corporations. Scientific and technical discovery was less hectic, and more subservient to the classical culture. Yet not even James Clerk Maxwell, the theorist of electricity and light, and an irrepressible punster, could have done better than Light Amplification by Stimulated Emission of Radiation, the modern Laser. How could we have believed in the exploits of Buck Rogers back in the thirties, when he didn't even know that this was the name of the 'death ray' pistol with which he set out to conquer the unfortunate inhabitants of exotic other worlds.

As in algebra, where x may one day stand for the height of a flag pole, and in the next problem be the weight of

an elephant, the context is all important. But really the interpretation of initials is very easy if you know what is being
talked about. I quote: 'At the meeting of the BNC' – that
would be the Bureau of Noxious Chemicals – 'held recently
at BNC' – everyone knows that's Brasenose College, Oxford
– 'the BNC' – clearly, the British Natrium Corporation –
'were represented by their chairman, BNC' – properly speaking, that's Sir Benedict Nortonson-Charlesworthy (though in
the trade he's usually called Big-Nosed Charlie). 'Concerning
the recent problems in the production of BNC' – that's *bi-
nitroso carbonyl*, of course – 'by the BNC process' – what is it
now? – oh, yes the Bloggs-Noguchi-Caruso process – very
delicate and explosive – 'he reported that the BNC' – the
Break-Neck Controller (probably the main safety device in
the plant) – 'had been accidentally put out of action by a
plumber's mate using a pair of BNC's' (ah, now there you've
got me – but it could be short for broad-nailed cutters – or is
it a block-neglecting cyclone – no, perhaps it's a black-naped
cormorant or even a bare-knifed candytuft). Well, you see,
I've proved my point, so I finish with those very initials:
'BNC, friends, BNC', which is the correct English translation
of *quod erat demonstrandum* which is Latin for QED, that is
'be not confused', friends, 'be not confused'.

Strings of formulae

The peculiar problem with physics is that it can't be stated
entirely in words. Physics is a science in which we attempt to
represent the phenomena of nature in mathematical form.
Without the machinery of number and quantity, symbol and
relationship, formal operation and logical necessity, it would
never have penetrated the atom or the galaxy. Writing up
physics in dictionary language is like trying to describe a
picture to a blind man.

For those of us who attempt to explain science to the

general public the problem is all too obvious. We are forced into desperate devices of metaphor, we skim lightly over vast areas of numerical data and algebraic analysis to give an impression of what we would be after. Mathematical argument is too strenuous and specialised for popularised science and we must simply do without it.

The interesting question, however, is whether mathematics should entirely dominate the exposition of physics in the technical scientific literature. Many theoretical physicists seem to think so. Their scientific papers consist of strings of formulae, linked with mechanical phrases.

Up to a point, such a style of exposition is honest and unambiguous. When he can't follow the text with full comprehension, the reader may himself take up paper and pencil and, if he has the mathematical dexterity to jump a few gaps of algebraic manipulation, then he will soon have the inestimable pleasure of participating in the thought processes of the writer, and being carried along to the same conclusions. Such writing is like a blue print, incomprehensible to the layman, which the skilful architect or engineer of mathematical physics can read constructively out of his own experience. To the expert there is real pleasure in grasping the inner harmonies of a well-expressed mathematical argument.

But I often get the impression that the authors of such papers live entirely within the abstract world of their own symbols. However compelling, however rigorous, a formal mathematical argument is not self-sufficient. Physics is about natural phenomena. To keep in touch with electrons and galaxies, magnetic fields and ocean waves, quarks and quanta and quasars, we need words, we must give them their own true names. Abstract symbols, x and y, alpha and omega, plus, minus and equals, have no permanent homes of their own in the human mind. To understand physics, to feel its concrete necessities, we must accept the material implications of grammatical sentences containing nouns and verbs, the words for things and actions. Einstein's equation, $E=mc^2$, carries little weight until we have said it aloud to ourselves: 'All mass is equivalent to energy; all energy has mass', and listen to the reverberations of these statements within our own understanding.

In writing up, or talking about physics, we must keep a thread of verbal reformulation and interpretation running in parallel with the mathematical formulae, and establish linkages crossing and recrossing the boundaries between these two modes of communication. Yet the two modes shouldn't be intermingled too closely, with equations and sentences jumbled together into a continuous text. Even for the mathematical physicist, verbal statements and symbolic relations don't occur within the same regions of the brain. We must beware of falling into a pidgin language where word and symbol, object and concept, are crudely compounded.

To convey the full meaning of physical thought, we need yet another mode of communication – visual imagery. 'One picture', they say, 'is worth a thousand words' – and can convey to the intuition the essence of a whole page of algebra. The innate capacity to manipulate and transform a diagram or a map, is one of the glorious powers of the human mind. But a map is useless unless its principal features are named. And there can be a great step forward in our understanding when we put a new name to a newly observed feature on such a map. Whatever other media or communication, whatever other languages we may bring to our aid, we cannot dispense altogether with words, with plain English, with didactic discourse, according to the rules of grammar, in telling each other about the physical world.

David Martin

Last words

This is my last *Words* and I am going to have a word about 'last words'. I don't suppose it will be the 'last word' in programmes about words but it is a last word I definitely intend to have. I intend having the last word because it is supposed to carry special authority. Not that I want my word to acquire the authority which belongs to the speech of dying men. Death is a heavy price to pay for authority.

Last words are the occasion of prophecy, of malediction and benediction. John of Gaunt in *Richard II* pronounces high benediction on this royal throne of Kings and malediction on Richard. He says:

> ' . . . the tongues of dying men
> Enforce attention like deep harmony . . . '

Last words are also a final will and testament. At the end a man is thought to have a special right to dispose of what is his and to name a successor. Concluding words are conclusive. The final word transfers the mantle of authority: 'and the mantle of Elijah fell upon Elisha'. This is the power of the succession: 'He has my dying voice'. There is an authoritative line and the last word is the link across the broken chain of death. Not a modern view perhaps but we keep a ghostly echo of it in the odd respect we pay a man's latest desires as compared with desires expressed in his prime.

A more modern last word is spoken at the end of radio discussion programmes. People are allowed a last, quick word to present the core of their argument. The real last word in these programmes is well worth having because the final impression is generally the one which counts. It's also an index of status. The last word and the final slot goes to the person of highest status. This is a powerful reinforcement of power. The reigning political party supports its reign by claiming the last programme; the Queen's first minister is allowed the last comment. The first is also the last: alpha is omega.

The last word gives you the advantage in personal battles. When a couple 'have words' a lot turns on who delivers the last load of verbal demolition. It's a vantage point for the next round. That's why 'words' between lovers and spouses go so many rounds. Proverbial wisdom says that the last word generally lies with the woman. She is supposed to have the word-craft to tie up her inarticulate, helplessly goaded man. Here the 'last word' may be compensation for lack of power. This is certainly so when the final comment is handed over to the weaker partner in a dispute. The question master says with kindly condescension 'I think perhaps X ought to have the last word, don't you?' But these are usually situations which don't matter. The respected and the powerful keep a tight hold on the right to a comeback.

One last kind of last word describes the best of its kind. A particular make of car is the last word in automobile design and a yacht is the last word in luxury. What is last is superlative.

My words run out. *My* last word should be a kind of benediction, a good word. Benedictions come at the end. The last is also the good. Last is good, best, final, definitive, compelling, powerful, memorable. It is goodbye and goodnight: end of relationship, end of day, end of life. Goodbye and goodnight are universal benedictions. In *Hamlet*, after the tragic play of 'words, words, words', comes 'Goodnight'.

'Goodnight sweet prince and flights of angels sing thee to thy rest . . .'

The rest is silence.

Biographical notes

Dannie Abse was born in 1923 at Cardiff. He is a doctor and works in a chest clinic in London though he returns to his home in Ogmore-by-Sea, Glamorgan, as much as he can. He has published six books of poetry and recently Hutchinson published his *Collected Poems* (May 1977). He has written, also, two autobiographical works, *Ash on a Young Man's Sleeve* (1954) and *A Poet in the Family* (1975) and has had several plays produced on both sides of the Atlantic. His most recent one, *Pythagoras*, was produced at the Birmingham Repertory Theatre in the autumn of 1976. He is married and has three children.

Robert Burchfield was born in Wanganui, New Zealand, in 1923, and was educated at Wanganui Technical College, Victoria University College (Wellington), and, as a Rhodes Scholar, at Magdalen College, Oxford. He is Chief Editor of the Oxford English Dictionaries and Fellow and Tutor in English Language at St Peter's College, Oxford. His publications include (with E. M. Burchfield) *The Land and People of New Zealand* (1953); (with C. T. Onions and G. W. S. Friedrichsen) *The Oxford Dictionary of English Etymology* (1966); A Supplement of Australian and New Zealand Words in the *Pocket Oxford Dictionary* (5th edn.) (1969); and *A Supplement to the Oxford English Dictionary*, Vol. I (A–G) (1972), Vol. II (H–N) (1976). He was awarded the CBE in 1975. He is now engaged on the compilation of Volume III (O–S) of *A Supplement to the Oxford English Dictionary*.

Robert Conquest was born in 1917 and was educated at Winchester College and Magdalen College, Oxford. He has held fellowships at several British and American universities, and been Literary Editor of the *Spectator*. In addition to several books of verse and fiction his works include a number on Soviet themes, among them *Power and Policy in the USSR* and *The Great Terror*.

Margaret Drabble was born in 1939 in Sheffield and educated at the Mount School, York, and Newham College, Cambridge. She married in 1960 and has two sons and one daughter. Her publications include *A Summer Birdcage* (1963); *The Waterfall* (1969);

The Needle's Eye (1972); and *The Realms of Gold* (1975). A new novel, *The Ice Age,* will appear later in 1977. She teaches Adult Education one day a week at Morley College.

Christopher Driver was born in 1932 and was educated at the Dragon School, Rugby School, and Christ Church, Oxford, where he read Greats. He became editor of the *Good Food Guide* in 1969, after eight years on the *Guardian,* and remains a freelance writer and broadcaster. He has published *A Future for the Free Churches?* (1962); *The Disarmers* (1964); and *The Exploding University* (1970). He is secretary of Highgate United Reformed Church in north London, and his interests include playing the violin and owning a secondhand bookshop.

D. J. Enright was born in 1920 and educated at Leamington College and Downing College, Cambridge. He taught for some twenty years, mostly in the Far East, and at present works in publishing. His publications include *Memoirs of a Mendicant Professor* (1969); *Shakespeare and the Students* (1970); *The Terrible Shears,* poems (1973); *Sad Ires,* poems (1975); *The Joke Shop,* a story for children (1976).

Stephen Hearst was born in 1919 and educated in Vienna, at Reading University and Brasenose College, Oxford. Now Controller of Radio 3, he is a writer and producer of television documentaries and arts features and was Head of Arts Features, BBC television, before assuming his present post. In 1961 he was seconded to the United Nations for a year to make films about underdevelopment and subsequently wrote a book on this subject under the title *Two Thousand Million Poor.*

David Martin was born in 1929 and was educated at Richmond and East Sheen Grammar School and at Westminster College, London. While teaching he studied sociology for a London external degree and was awarded the university studentship to do postgraduate study at the London School of Economics. He is now Professor of Sociology at the London School of Economics, and his publications include *Pacifism* (1965); *A Sociology of English Religion* (1967); *The Religious and the Secular* (1969); *Tracts against the Times* (1973); and *A General Theory of Secularisation* (1977). He was Cadbury Lecturer in Birmingham University in 1973 and Ferguson Lecturer in Manchester University in 1977. He is currently working on the sociology of music.

Chaim Raphael's writing reflects two sides of his experience—as an academic and civil servant. Before the war, he was Cowley Lecturer in Hebrew, and Kennicott Fellow, at Oxford. Wartime and postwar service for the Government in the USA was followed by a long spell in Whitehall as head of the Information Division of the Treasury, after which, in 1969, he returned to academic life as a Research Fellow at the University of Sussex. His books include *Memoirs of a Special Case* (1962); *The Walls of Jerusalem* (1968); and *A Feast of History* (1972). Under the pseudonym Jocelyn Davey, he has also written a series of thrillers, the latest of which – *A Treasury Alarm* – was published in 1976.

Frederic Raphael was born in Chicago in 1931. His family moved to this country seven years later and he was educated at Charterhouse and St John's College, Cambridge. He is married and has three children. His novels include *The Limits of Love; Lindmann; Orchestra and Beginners; Like Men Betrayed; April, June & November; Richard's Things;* and *California Time.* He is also the author of *Somerset Maugham & His World.* He has written a number of screenplays, including *Nothing But The Best; Darling; Two For The Road;* and *Far From The Madding Crowd.* His television scripts include *Rogue Male* and *The Glittering Prizes.* He is a frequent broadcaster and a regular contributor to the book pages of *The Sunday Times.* He is also a Fellow of the Royal Society of Literature. He is at present engaged on a new translation and adaptation for BBC television of the *Oresteia of Aeschylus.*

Cardew Robinson, actor, entertainer and writer, who was born in Goodmayes, Essex, and educated at Harrow Grammar School, first became known to the public in the 1950s with his famous schoolboy character, 'Cardew the Cad of St Fanny's', in variety, radio, television and films. The character was also immortalised in the children's comic paper *Radio Fun.* Since then his continued activity as an actor and comedian in all these media has run parallel with his work as a writer of short stories, articles, songs, and television and radio scripts. He has published two books, *How to be a Failure,* and (with Alban Greaves) *The ABC of the Panto People.*

Ian Robinson was educated at King Edward VI Grammar School, Retford, and Downing College, Cambridge (under F. R. Leavis) and since 1961 has been a lecturer in English at University College, Swansea. His first book, *Chaucer's Prosody,* had been rejected when submitted for PhD so he is plain **Mr.** Later publications include *The Survival of English, The New Grammarians' Funeral* and (while Mr Heath was still leader of the Conservative Party) *The Decline and Fall of Mr Heath.* He edited the quarterly review *The Human World* for most of its brief life (1970–74). He is currently at work on an effort to extend into our times the tradition of judgment of civilisation found in the work of Carlyle and Arnold, and on a book on the relationship between imagination and prose in the English novel.

Vernon Scannell was born in 1922. His poetry has been awarded The Heinemann Award for Literature (1960) and The Cholmondoley Poetry Prize (1974). Elected a Fellow of the Royal Society of Literature (1960). Most recent publications include *The Loving Game* (choice of the Poetry Book Society) and *Not Without Glory,* a critical study of second world war poetry.

Kenneth Tynan was born in Birmingham in 1923. After receiving a degree in English Literature from Oxford, he directed for the English theatre and television. He joined the *Spectator* in 1951 as drama critic, and subsequently served in the same capacity on the *Evening Standard* and then the *Daily Sketch* before joining *The Observer.* He took a leave of absence from *The Observer* between 1958 and 1960 to act as drama critic for *The New Yorker.* At the invitation of Sir Laurence Olivier, he joined the National Theatre in 1963 as its first literary manager, a post he held until 1973. In 1969 he compiled and part-wrote *Oh! Calcutta,* which ran for three years in New York and is now in the seventh year of its London run. Tynan is the author of the following books: *He That Plays the King; Alec Guinness; Persona Grata; Bull Fever; Curtains; Tynan Right and Left; A View of the English Stage; The Sound of Two Hands Clapping.* He is a Fellow of the Royal Society of Literature.

Mary Warnock was born in 1924, and was educated at St Swithin's School, Winchester, and Lady Margaret Hall, Oxford. She was a fellow and tutor in philosophy at St Hugh's College, Oxford, until 1966, then for six years Headmistress at Oxford High School. Since then she has had a research fellowship at Lady Margaret Hall, and now at St Hugh's College. Her books include *Ethics since* 1900 (1960); *The Philosophy of J. P. Sartre* (1963); *Existentialism* (1970); and *Imagination* (1976). She is currently writing on the philosophy of education.

J. G. Weightman was born in 1915 and educated at Hexham Grammar School and the Universities of Durham and Poitiers. From 1939 to 1950, he worked in the French Service of the BBC, as an announcer, translator and programme assistant. Since 1950, he has been a teacher of French in the University of London, specialising in the literature of the 18th and the 20th centuries; he is now Professor of French at Westfield College. With his wife, J. D. Weightman, he has produced a number of translations, including *Tristes Tropiques* by Claude Levi-Strauss. In 1973, he published a collection of essays on modernism, *The Concept of the Avant-Garde*.

John Ziman was born in 1925 and was brought up in New Zealand. He studied mathematics and physics at Oxford and was a Lecturer at the Cavendish Laboratory and a Fellow of Kings College, Cambridge, until he became Professor of Theoretical Physics at the University of Bristol in 1964. In addition to scientific papers and books on the theory of metals and semi-conductors he is the author of *Camford Observed* (jointly with Jasper Rose) (1964); *Public Knowledge* (1968); and *The Force of Knowledge* (1976). He has been a Fellow of the Royal Society since 1967 and is Chairman of the Council for Science and Society.